Thinking Like
Mathematicians

· ·

Thinking Like Mathematicians

· ·

Putting the NCTM
Standards into Practice

Updated for Standards 2000

THOMAS ROWAN
BARBARA BOURNE

HEINEMANN
Portsmouth, NH

Heinemann
A division of Reed Elsevier Inc.
361 Hanover Street
Portsmouth, NH 03801-3912
www.heinemann.com

Offices and agents throughout the world

© 1994, 2001 by Thomas Rowan and Barbara Bourne

The author and publisher wish to thank those who have generously given permission to reprint borrowed material:
Excerpts from *Principles and Standards for School Mathematics* by the National Council of Teachers of Mathematics. Copyright © 2000 by the National Council of Teachers of Mathematics. Reprinted by permission. All rights reserved.

Library of Congress Cataloging-in-Publication Data
Rowan, Thomas E.
    Thinking like mathematicians : putting the NCTM standards into practice / Thomas Rowan, Barbara Bourne.—Updated for standards 2000.
        p. cm.
    Includes bibliographical references.
    ISBN 0-325-00347-5
    1. Mathematics—Study and teaching (Elementary). I. Bourne, Barbara. II. Title.

QA135.5 .R72 2001
372.7—dc21

                                                                    00-046123

Editor: Victoria Merecki
Production: Lynne Reed
Cover design: Darci Mehall, Aureo Design
Manufacturing: Deanna Richardson

Printed in the United States of America on acid-free paper
04 03 02 01 00   VP   1 2 3 4 5

Contents

ACKNOWLEDGMENTS   vi

1
MATH POWER   1

2
DIRECTIONS FOR CHANGE: THE NCTM STANDARDS   6

3
CHILDREN CONSTRUCTING KNOWLEDGE   21

4
TEACHERS AS PROBLEM SOLVERS   30

5
BUILDING UNDERSTANDING   38

6
DEVELOPING A PLAN   54

7
IMPLEMENTING THE PROGRAM   74

8
EVALUATION   101

9
THE CASE OF ONE YOUNG MATHEMATICIAN   119

10
SOME QUESTIONS ANSWERED   126

WORKS CITED   151

Acknowledgments

The authors wish to thank the children, parents, teachers, principals, and other school system staff who have given their permission and support to the publication of this book. In particular, teachers Chris Oberdorf, Maura Backenstoe, Jill Hudson, and Patty Hughes allowed classroom observations. Patty Hughes, Chris Perretti, Leona Arthur, and Jill Hudson allowed photographs to be taken in their classrooms. The photographer for the Montgomery County Public Schools, William Mills, took all of the excellent photographs.

Project IMPACT, on which the book is based, was supported in part by the National Science Foundation. The opinions expressed are those of the authors and are not necessarily those of the National Science Foundation. We are most grateful for the support of the Project IMPACT staff, particularly Dr. Patricia Campbell, the project director.

We also thank the Montgomery County Public Schools for permitting us to observe and report on Project IMPACT.

Finally, we want to thank Toby Gordon, Victoria Merecki, and the staff at Heinemann for their excellent assistance and support while the original book and this revision were being developed and published.

MATH POWER

*A*nne Ikeda asked her kindergarten students how they could determine the number of **single** mittens that would be needed for every student in the class to have one pair of mittens.

After providing time for each child to work with a partner, Ms. Ikeda brought the children back together to share their ideas with the class.

Rosa was among the first to offer a plan of action. "I'm going to go around and tap everybody on the head and count," she said. Her teacher nodded. "Then I'm going to go around and do it again."

"Why will you go around a second time, Rosa?" asked Ms. Ikeda.

*"Well, because everyone has **two** hands!"*

* * * * * * *

Tyrone, a first grader, was handed seven sticks of unifix cubes, a pencil, and a sheet of paper with this problem:

$$68 - 50 = \square$$

Tyrone ignored the unifix cubes and, after only a few moments of thought, wrote the number 18 in the box.

"How did you do that, Tyrone? What was your thinking?" the teacher asked.

*"Well, I thought 50 plus 50 . . . ," began Tyrone, then stopped and thought. "No, no," he continued, "I thought 50 **minus** 50. That's 0. Then I said, that means there's 10 more to get to 60, and then 8 more to get to 68. The answer is 18."*

Rosa and Tyrone are thinking like mathematicians. They are not intimidated by math, nor are they overly concerned to hear the teacher say that their answers are correct. Each is confident, creative, and actively involved in the math process. In fact, at this early point in time, Rosa and Tyrone are well on the road to realizing their "math power."

Math power. Another trendy phrase? More educational jargon? Not to those who work with Rosa and Tyrone, for despite the children's high-level thinking skills, success in math could be out of their reach. Each attends an elementary school on the outskirts of a large city where, as in many similar schools, the test scores are usually quite low. The odds are against high academic achievement in urban neighborhoods with low income and inadequate resources. Teachers must address and accommodate for the variety of complex academic and social issues that confront their students and are left little time for recognizing and supporting the thinking skills of individual children. But since empowering children in mathematics has become an increasingly important component in both children's schools, Rosa and Tyrone could beat the odds. Their teachers have found that planning instruction based on their students' thinking pays dividends in student achievement as well as overall classroom atmosphere.

Originally, Rosa's and Tyrone's teachers changed their teaching strategies and math curriculums to align with the goals of the National Council of Teachers of Mathematics' *Curriculum and Evaluation Standards for School Mathematics,* published in 1989. More recently, NCTM published *Principles and Standards for School Mathematics* (2000), a document that clarifies and expands on the earlier one. Both standards documents recommend fundamental revisions to the way most mathematics instruction has been routinely implemented in American classrooms.

The 1989 standards established five basic goals for students:

1. learning to value mathematics
2. becoming confident in their ability to do mathematics
3. becoming mathematical problem solvers
4. learning to communicate mathematically
5. learning to reason mathematically (5–6)

The continuing importance of these goals is evident throughout the *Principles and Standards* document, especially as the "Learning Principle" is discussed:

> Students who memorize facts and procedures without understanding often are not sure when or how to use what they know. (20)

> A major goal of school mathematics programs is to create autonomous learners, and learning with understanding supports this goal. (21)

When challenged with appropriately chosen tasks, students become confident in their ability to tackle difficult problems, eager to figure things out on their own, flexible in exploring mathematical ideas and trying alternative solution paths, and willing to persevere. (21)

The NCTM *Principles and Standards for School Mathematics*, using the latest research on mathematics learning, as well as research into how the human brain works, emphasizes the need to provide children with opportunities to construct for themselves a solid mathematical foundation. This view arises, in part, from the assumption that an understanding of children's intellectual, social, and emotional development should drive the elementary curriculum. Children need to continually interact with their environment, constructing, modifying, and integrating ideas. Placing students in carefully planned situations provides opportunities that extend natural modes of learning to benefit the growth of mathematical ideas.

In classrooms that focus on the goals of the NCTM standards, children like Rosa and Tyrone are encouraged to build their math power. They do not sit passively, listening to a teacher who controls the way they do math, nor do they watch quietly while a few highly verbal children dominate class discussions. They spend little time memorizing arithmetical algorithms and rules that they don't understand. Instead, they create or adapt procedures that they do understand and can use efficiently. These students are provided with multiple situations that build, and build on, their mathematical backgrounds and personal interests. Students in these classrooms are allowed to solve problems in ways that are meaningful to them: they work cooperatively with their peers; use a variety of manipulatives; receive guidance through insightful teacher questioning; and have ample time and opportunity for thought, reflection, and discourse. Consequently, the children see themselves as doers of mathematics —as mathematicians.

These classrooms are rarely quiet, but instead hum with the sounds of small voices sharing experiences and ideas. As children work in small groups, they are able to collaborate on shared activity—explaining, debating, defending, negotiating, evaluating, and eventually concurring—in a collegial atmosphere. Large-group meetings provide forums to air alternative solutions and to decide on the correct solution. Teachers regularly ask, "Did anyone do this a different way?" until each unique method is unearthed. In listening to classmates explain how they arrived at an answer, students learn to value the

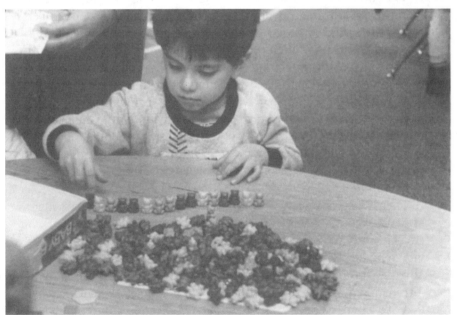

Children in classrooms that implement the NCTM standards have many opportunities to make sense of mathematics.

thinking of their peers and quickly discover that there is no one correct way to "do math."

Because their teachers value *thinking* as much as *answers*, these students are increasingly willing to persist, participate, and share. They can be certain that every idea will be treated with respect and that they will be allowed to complete their explanation without interruption. Students' processes and solutions are rarely wrong, although some may address questions other than the one currently under investigation. More often than not, when asked to explain how they got a solution, these students recognize and correct for themselves any errors they have made. If they do not self-correct, their explanation usually gives the teacher insights into misunderstandings that guide the formulation of questions to help the children see and correct their own errors.

Teachers are discovering that the benefits of this type of program are not confined to mathematics alone. As active participants in the processes of math, students incorporate the expressive and receptive components of communication—listening, speaking, reading, and writing—thereby augmenting and enhancing their basic language skills. In these math environments, children think, talk, write, and even model or draw out their mathematics expressions. At the same time, they must actively attend to the ideas of others in order to debate and negotiate shared solutions.

The interaction of mathematics and language has proven beneficial to other content areas as well. The same kind of thinking that is recommended by the NCTM standards—to understand, communicate, and use mathematics—also serves as a powerful tool for interpreting information, visualizing concepts, and implementing solutions in subjects such as social studies, science, and art.

Classrooms where the NCTM standards are taken seriously empower students by enabling them to feel that they are in control of the mathematics rather than that the mathematics is in control of them. Problem-solving tasks move from traditional textbook-driven, formulaic problems to encounters with real-life situations that inspire creative solutions. Children instinctively see the value of mathematics as they make connections between it and the real world. They begin to reason mathematically and communicate their ideas through the language of math. Most important, because they are constructing their own knowledge, children become confident in their ability to meet the challenge. They are mathematicians.

2

·······

DIRECTIONS FOR CHANGE: THE NCTM STANDARDS

One episode of the comic strip "Calvin and Hobbes" suggested that math is like a religion because you have to accept its ideas and results on faith. "No one can say how it happens," Calvin explains. "You either believe it or you don't."

Unfortunately, many students (and adults) share Calvin's philosophy. They view mathematics as a set of unfathomable rules to memorize, be tested on, and eventually forget. Many adults instill in children the belief that only the "whiz kids," the "Einsteins," have the innate ability to understand the logic and processes of mathematics, and admit that they, too, don't view themselves as "good" in mathematics.

You don't have to look too far beyond the newspaper comics to see the need for a change in attitude toward mathematics. Both the reality and the perception of poor student achievement are well documented. Some have called it a crisis. Scores on both national and international tests appear to get lower as students progress through school. Colleges report large numbers of students taking remedial mathematics upon entry. Business leaders claim that many students entering the American workforce are ill prepared to meet the demands of the workplace, and many adults wonder whether students will be ready for the advanced technological nature of the society into which they will graduate. Indeed, references to the problems in American schools, particularly in mathematics and science, are frequently the subject of discussion in the news media.

In the early 1980s, several national reports warned parents and educators of an impending educational crisis. Reports such as *A Nation at Risk* (1983) and *Educating Americans for the Twenty-First*

Century (1983) documented many of the problems facing our schools and called for reform.

Americans were further alarmed when international achievement results indicated that many of our students perform less successfully in mathematics than students educated in other countries, many of which are less wealthy and less technologically advanced than the United States. In comparison to students from other nations that participated in the testing, the relative performance of American students was average at fourth grade, considerably lower at eighth grade, and lower still at twelfth grade (Schmidt et al. 1997). While many explanations were offered for this apparent decline, some have interpreted it to indicate that American students enter school capable of high mathematics achievement, but are unable to capitalize on that potential because of the manner in which mathematics is currently taught in most schools (Carpenter and Moser 1983).

The greatest disparities in achievement between American students and those from higher-scoring nations appear to be in the areas of critical thinking—problem solving and mathematical reasoning. (Tests given entirely within the United States confirm the imbalance favoring skills and computation.) Such test results, coupled with the increased importance of technology in today's economy, led scientific and educational leaders in the United States to call for drastic action to improve the teaching of science and mathematics.

In 1986, the NCTM responded to the challenge by appointing the Commission on Standards for School Mathematics to create a vision of mathematical literacy and develop a set of national standards to guide schools towards that vision. The resulting document (*Curriculum and Evaluation Standards for School Mathematics* [1989]) was the most significant response to date to the call for improving mathematics teaching and learning. (The first NCTM document was followed by a second, *Professional Standards for Teaching Mathematics* [1990], and a third, *Assessment Standards for School Mathematics* [1995].)

In 1997, the Council appointed a commission to plan and direct a representative group of mathematics educators and mathematicians to update the standards to reflect an increased understanding of how children learn and to better meet the demands of a diverse community of learners. The commission established a twenty-seven-member writing team for the revision process, including representation from across the United States and Canada. This team included mathematics educators and mathematicians from all levels, prekindergarten to college, from both public and private schools.

Production of the 1989 *Standards* and then the *Principles and Standards for School Mathematics* (2000) were significant commitments by NCTM to rigorous and time-consuming processes. The Council is committed to giving guidance to the establishment of mathematics programs that will meet the needs of all students. Research into the teaching and learning of mathematics was thoroughly reviewed by the writers as each document was developed.

DO WE NEED NATIONAL STANDARDS?

National standards—the very concept raises questions for American parents and educators who have grown up believing in the autonomy of independent school districts. What exactly are national standards? Are they really necessary or is this just an excuse for more educational mandates: a different set of rules and regulations; a national test that must be "taught to"? And just what is the difference between national standards and a national curriculum; between standards and standardization?

On April 26, 1992, President Keith Geiger of the National Education Association (NEA) referred in his "Message from the President" to national educational standards as "statements of quality" directing school improvement. The term *national standards*, he said, does not imply developing a national curriculum—or national test. Unlike a curriculum, which spells out content scope and sequence and specific learning outcomes, standards are broad, far-reaching goals that establish a direction in which education should point.

True to this definition, the NCTM *Principles and Standards* is indeed broad in scope. Rather than isolating and prescribing specific content grade by grade, the standards use a four-section format, dividing the recommendations among four broad grade ranges, grades pre-K–2, 3–5, 6–8, and 9–12. Within each band the standards are presented and described so that an instructional philosophy is communicated along with the content goals. Ten broad standards establish content and process goals spanning prekindergarten through grade 12:

Number and Operations
Instructional programs from prekindergarten through grade 12 should enable all students to:
- understand numbers, ways of representing numbers, relationships among numbers, and number systems;

- understand meanings of operations and how they relate to one another;
- compute fluently and make reasonable estimates.

Algebra

Instructional programs from prekindergarten through grade 12 should enable all students to:

- understand patterns, relations, and functions;
- represent and analyze mathematical situations and structures using algebraic symbols;
- use mathematical models to represent and understand quantitative relationships;
- analyze change in various contexts.

Geometry

Instructional programs from prekindergarten through grade 12 should enable all students to:

- analyze characteristics and properties of two- and three-dimensional shapes and develop mathematical arguments about geometric relationships;
- specify locations and describe spatial relationships using coordinate geometry and other representational systems;
- apply transformations and use symmetry to analyze mathematical situations;
- use visualization, spatial reasoning, and geometric modeling to solve problems.

Measurement

Instructional programs from prekindergarten through grade 12 should enable all students to:

- understand measurable attributes of objects and the units, systems, and processes of measurement;
- apply appropriate techniques, tools, and formulas to determine measurements.

Data Analysis and Probability

Instructional programs from prekindergarten through grade 12 should enable all students to:

- formulate questions that can be addressed with data and collect, organize, and display relevant data to answer them;
- select and use appropriate statistical methods to analyze data;
- develop and evaluate inferences and predictions that are based on data;
- understand and apply basic concepts of probability.

Problem Solving

Instructional programs from prekindergarten through grade 12 should enable all students to:

- build new mathematical knowledge through problem solving;
- solve problems that arise in mathematics and in other contexts;
- apply and adapt a variety of strategies to solve problems;
- monitor and reflect on the process of mathematical problem solving.

Reasoning and Proof
Instructional programs from prekindergarten through grade 12 should enable all students to:
- recognize reasoning and proof as fundamental aspects of mathematics;
- make and investigate mathematical conjectures;
- develop and evaluate mathematical arguments and proofs;
- select and use various types of reasoning and methods of proof.

Communication
Instructional programs from prekindergarten through grade 12 should enable all students to:
- organize and consolidate their mathematical thinking through communication;
- communicate their mathematical thinking coherently and clearly to peers, teachers, and others;
- analyze and evaluate the mathematical thinking and strategies of others;
- use the language of mathematics to express mathematical ideas precisely.

Connections
Instructional programs from prekindergarten through grade 12 should enable all students to:
- recognize and use connections among mathematical ideas;
- understand how mathematical ideas interconnect and build on one another to produce a coherent whole;
- recognize and apply mathematics in contexts outside of mathematics.

Representation
Instructional programs from prekindergarten through grade 12 should enable all students to:
- create and use representations to organize, record, and communicate mathematical ideas;
- select, apply, and translate among mathematical representations to solve problems;
- use representations to model and interpret physical, social, and mathematical phenomena.
  (NCTM 2000)

DIRECTIONS OF CHANGE

The NCTM commission and the standards writers were concerned with identifying basic math concepts and attitudes that need to be fostered in all children, but the foundation for their recommendations was knowledge of, and commitment to, how students learn and, more specifically, how they learn mathematics.

While the need for change seems obvious to most, some find the recommendations a radical departure from the traditional system. Most agree, however, that the *Principles and Standards*, like the *Curriculum and Evaluation Standards* that preceded it, sets out a plan that is exciting, challenging, and clearly committed to students and their individual growth in mathematics. Because the essential message of the two standards documents is the same, this text will refer to them simply as "the NCTM standards."

Schools committed to incorporating the NCTM standards need to rethink long-established modes of classroom operation. To this end, the writers have provided a clear direction for change, calling for modification of some deeply ensconced classroom routines. Memorization of "math facts" in ways that are devoid of meaning and that heighten anxiety in children must be replaced with strategies that enable children to remember these number combinations with understanding and confidence. By using a known fact that is related, these strategies can be used to quickly recall a forgotten fact.

Teaching methods that promote rote memorization of single algorithms should give way to strategies that encourage students to invent, and later refine, their own ways to solve problems. Student-invented procedures may eventually lead to "traditional" algorithms, but only if those algorithms make sense to the student and are clearly more efficient than the student's own procedures. Algebraic thinking should begin in prekindergarten and should grow gradually across all of the school years. Students should be allowed to solve problems in ways that make sense to them, using pencil and paper or manipulative materials. The written procedures should always be a way of recording, rather than replacing, thinking. Above all, the mathematics that they do should make sense to students.

For some, these new ideas will be a drastic change from established classroom routines, a step into a whole new sphere of teaching practice. Others will recognize familiar themes that they already incorporate into their classroom programs. But most will find common ground—a collective starting point—in NCTM's basic goals, expecting students to value mathematics, be confident in their own abilities, be mathematical problem solvers, and communicate and reason mathematically.

The standards documents never recommend omitting specific informational knowledge from the mathematics curriculum. Instead, they suggest a reevaluation of mathematics processes, procedures, and emphases in the classroom. The following powerful statement can guide the nature of mathematics instruction:

> "Knowing" mathematics is "doing" mathematics. A person gathers, discovers or creates knowledge in the course of some activity having a purpose. This active process is different from mastering concepts and procedures. We do not assert that informational knowledge has no value, only that its value lies in the extent to which it is useful in the course of some purposeful activity. (NCTM *Curriculum and Evaluation Standards,* 7)

The *Principles and Standards* reinforces this view:

> Well-chosen tasks can pique students' curiosity and draw them into mathematics. The tasks may be connected to the real-world experiences of students, or they may arise in contexts that are purely mathematical. Regardless of the context, worthwhile tasks should be intriguing, with a level of challenge that invites speculation and hard work. (NCTM *Principles and Standards,* 19)

MATHEMATICS IN THE PRIMARY GRADES

In addressing the specific needs of primary-grade children, the standards documents make several important assertions about children and how they can best achieve the characteristics described in the overall goals—characteristics that define children as young mathematicians. The *Principles and Standards* suggests characteristics such as the following (pp. 75–7 and 143–6):

1. Most students enter school confident in their own abilities, and they are confident and eager to learn more about numbers and mathematical objects. This confidence should be nurtured and built upon as instruction is planned. Children need opportunities to create their own methods of problem solving and the assurance that their teachers and peers will value their thinking as creative and viable. Success for all students is integral to the goals of any mathematics program, so teachers must recognize and accommodate for a variety of student talents, challenges, and learning styles, as well as for the complex needs of a diverse student population.

2. Programs should build on and extend students' intuitive and informal mathematics knowledge, be grounded in knowledge of child development, and take place in environments that encourage students to be active learners and accept new challenges. Children enter school with the ingredients essential to budding mathematicians—a variety of life experiences from which they can draw context for learning, a well-developed vocabulary (although it may not be English), and best of all, a highly tuned sense of curiosity. When mathematics programs begin with these strengths, newly acquired concepts take root easily and form a system that is sufficiently strong to support additional learning. A developmentally appropriate curriculum recognizes that children are naturally social, active, and curious and need to explore new ideas in safe, enjoyable, and stimulating environments.

3. Effective teachers know how to ask questions and build lessons that reveal students' prior knowledge; they can then design experiences and lessons that respond to, and build on, this knowledge. The goal of the math program should be to build understanding rather than to have students memorize many rules that may or may not be understood or retained in memory. Constructing understanding requires students to make connections between new information and previous learning. By asking probing questions that uncover students' thinking, teachers can plan instruction that encourages children to make these connections. These questions will also help the teacher assess whether students are making connections and gaining real understanding, not just memorizing procedures and definitions.

4. All students can learn significant mathematics and teachers should set high expectations for the mathematics learning of students. High expectations are realized when teachers let their students know that they are capable of solving math problems, when teachers provide problems in which children use their background knowledge to solve these problems, and when they provide adequate time for student thinking. Furthermore, when students' ideas are valued and shared openly in an atmosphere that fosters success, they will begin to set high expectations for themselves.

5. Children learn by talking about what they are thinking and doing and by collaborating and sharing their ideas with others.

Children should have sufficient time to inquire, explore, discuss, and revisit ideas so that they can build deep conceptual understanding. When the classroom atmosphere is one in which children know that their creative ideas and ways of solving are at least as valued as the answers, they are willing and anxious to be creative and inventive. Then they can work seriously in pairs or small groups to solve problems, share strategies, and then to discuss their ideas in the large group setting. Classrooms in which the focus is on getting the answer and moving on do not foster this atmosphere and therefore do not encourage students to think like mathematicians.

6. Children must be actively involved in doing mathematics. They must interact with the physical world and with other children and supportive adults. For children just developing the ability to think abstractly, concrete materials can provide a bridge to, and foundation for, that thinking. Mathematics is not a "spectator sport." Hands-on activity can be critical to "doing" mathematics, and the basic language components—speaking, listening, reading, and writing—serve as necessary links between action and mathematical understanding.

7. Children should see how mathematics is applied in other subjects and in daily activities. Children will value mathematics as an essential life tool when they see it incorporated throughout the curriculum. Mathematics helps to make meaning out of other content areas, specifically science and social studies. However, its application should not be restricted to academic disciplines. Classrooms offering strong mathematical programs will apply concepts through incidental daily routines and activities.

8. A broad range of content should be taught. Programs that put too much emphasis on computational skills at the expense of other areas of mathematics provide an imbalanced mathematics curriculum. Math can be engaging to students, for it is far more than memorized facts, rules, and procedures. Children need to apply mathematical concepts as they explore, develop, test, and describe ideas that help them make sense of their world. The noncomputational areas of mathematics often appeal to students who are slower at developing computational proficiency, and can provide connections that motivate and form the basis for increased computational proficiency.

Figure 2–1
CALCULATOR ACTIVITY

Overview
This popular paper-and-pencil activity that helps children to build an understanding of the base ten number system becomes even more powerful when students use calculators. Students use four randomly selected digits to create a number as close as possible to a target number. In the paper/pencil version of the activity the students simply draw four blank lines on paper and plug in each digit as it is read. A digit cannot be moved after it is placed. When played with calculators, the students must enter each digit into the calculator without changing any digit that was previously placed. This causes the student to have to think, for example, of a 9 as 9,000 if that 9 is to be placed in the thousands place of the calculator.

Level
Second and third grade

Grouping
Individuals

Materials
Calculators for each child/pair
Ten cards, number 0–9

Procedure
- Establish a target number: the greatest number possible when four digits are combined, or the least number possible when those numbers are combined.
- The teacher or student leader shuffles a set of cards that contains the ten digits 0–9.
- One at a time, four cards are drawn and read aloud. They are not replaced after they are drawn.
- As each digit is drawn students decide which place they want it to hold and enter the digit accordingly.

For example,
The teacher or the class decides that the target is the least number possible made with the four digits.
The first digit drawn is a 2.
Because its value is so low, the student decides to place the 2 in the thousands place.
To enter the digit on the calculator she must enter + 2000 =.
The next digit drawn is a 5.
The student decides to place the 5 in the tens place.
To enter this digit on the calculator she must enter + 50 =.
The screen will then show 2050.
The next number drawn must either be placed in the ones or the hundreds place. If the number is 7, 8, or 9, she will probably decide to place it in the ones place. If, on the other hand, the next number drawn is a 0, 1, or 3, she will probably decide to place it in the hundreds place.

Extensions
- Have students play this game in pairs and discuss their strategies.
- After whole-group practice, set this game up as a "center" activity.

9. Programs should take advantage of technology. Calculators and computers can support mathematics instruction and enhance understanding (see Figure 2–1 on p. 15). All students, beginning with those in the primary grades, should learn to use these tools responsibly. Research has shown that children who are in classrooms that use calculators appropriately benefit from that use. They score better on tests that do not allow the calculator to be used than students who are in classrooms that do not use calculators. Although computers and calculators add a dimension to the instructional program that could not be achieved with pencil and paper alone, students should recognize that, often, mental computation is far more efficient and powerful than that performed on a calculator. Technology provides a means for students to investigate patterns and algorithms in ways that motivate and encourage deeper thinking than might otherwise occur. Instructional activities that use calculators and computers often help students better understand the mathematics.

What a radical departure this is from traditional assumptions about learners and their environments! These assumptions focus on the nature of the students and the interaction of the students with the mathematics, rather than on some artificial analysis of traditional content. They incorporate documented research about the growth and development of young children in determining what to teach and how to teach it. They recognize that real mathematics is dynamic and process oriented, rather than static and answer oriented.

Classrooms that adopt these premises will be active places where teachers pay constant attention to how well children are making sense of the mathematics being studied. To facilitate this process, programs will incorporate what the children have experienced outside of the school setting so that new ideas can be learned with understanding, and they will allow children to construct their own mathematics knowledge through such activities.

The two NCTM standards documents are not simply theory and rhetoric. To help teachers achieve both the content and the spirit of the documents, they provide background information and examples of appropriate mathematics activities. The first five standards specify the content strands that are to be taught. Standards 6–10 represent broad processes for empowering children in mathematics. Accompanying each standard are discussions and suggested activities to help teachers accomplish the intended outcomes.

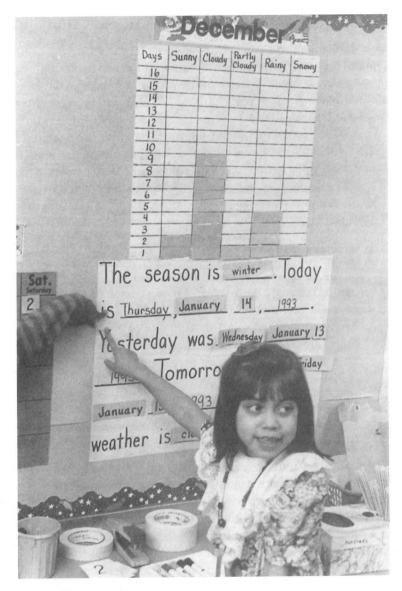

The NCTM standards advocate incorporating mathematics into many daily activities.

PUTTING THE NCTM STANDARDS INTO PRACTICE

When implementing the NCTM standards, teachers are encouraged to incorporate several distinct elements into the mathematics program. They informally assess student progress throughout the day and take care to value each child's learning style and individual approach to math problems. Teachers provide opportunities for children to solve problems in meaningful situations; use manipulative materials; develop their own procedures to solve math problems; talk about the mathematics they are using; and encounter math throughout their curriculum—in language and reading, social studies and science, art, and physical education.

Activities that are developmentally appropriate reflect children's need to actively interact with their physical and social environments in order to develop intellectually, socially, and emotionally (see Figure 2–2). Hands-on experiences and those activities that appeal to children's natural curiosity tap a sense of inquiry in children and serve to stimulate discovery and mathematics learning.

But hands-on activity, in and of itself, is not enough. Children must make connections—connecting their classroom experiences with prior experiences and connecting these with mathematics concepts. Communication activities, discussions with classmates and teachers, and writing about math experiences help students make these connections. Without such discourse, the hands-on process may actually become an alternate way to get answers that is not connected to the mathematics they are trying to learn. When students begin to write mathematical sentences, using numerals and symbols for operations and equality, those written symbols should be simply a way of recording what they did. In traditional programs the procedures often replace thinking for many children, but in standards-based instruction the written expressions, whether in words or mathematical symbols, are a way of *expressing* thinking, not a *replacement* for thinking.

The NCTM standards recommend that teachers use mathematics throughout the school day, as well as foster its incorporation into take-home activities. A good way to help children see how mathematics is applied in other subjects and in the real world is to call attention to these applications across the curriculum. These need not, and should not, be restricted to academic content areas. Daily routines such as recording attendance, calendar activity, and assigning classroom chores are rife with mathematics potential.

Most children arrive at school with the tools necessary for suc-

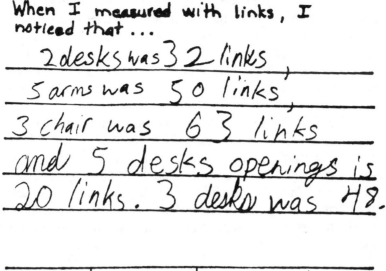

When I measured with links, I noticed that . . .

2 desks was 32 links,
5 arms was 50 links,
3 chair was 63 links
and 5 desks openings is 20 links. 3 desks was 48.

$$
\begin{array}{r} 16 \\ + 16 \\ \hline 32 \end{array}
\qquad
\begin{array}{r} 10 \\ 10 \\ 10 \\ + 10 \\ 10 \\ \hline 50 \end{array}
\qquad
\begin{array}{r} 21 \\ 21 \\ + 21 \\ \hline 63 \end{array}
\qquad
\begin{array}{r} 4 \\ 4 \\ 4 \\ + 4 \\ 4 \\ \hline 20 \end{array}
$$

Figure 2–2 *The NCTM standards recommend using opportunities for children to interact with their environments and connect their experiences with mathematics concepts.*

cess—curiosity, communication skills, and a variety of life experiences. Upon entering school, young children are able to solve problems that call for computational skills they have not yet learned. However, after several years of traditional mathematics instruction, they become less creative and rely on memorized procedures. The result: their problem-solving skills and performance actually drop (Carpenter and Moser 1983). This is consistent with the results of several international assessments. American students performed better in computational skills than in problem solving and reasoning. And in one international assessment, the Third International Mathematics and Science Survey (TIMSS), the higher the grade level tested, the lower the American students' comparative level of performance.

Mathematics programs that implement the NCTM standards

THINKING LIKE MATHEMATICIANS

encourage teachers to provide children with opportunities to share experiences from outside the school and connect those with the mathematics that is being learned within the school. This does not happen automatically. Children must be encouraged and given time to relate school mathematics to their personal experience through personal reflection, student-student discussions, and student-teacher discussions.

Children in the United States have the same intellectual capacities as any other children around the world; there is no reason to believe that any geographic area or ethnic culture has a corner on innate mathematical ability. As classrooms adopt techniques that encourage students to retain and apply the skills with which they enter school and construct their own mathematical procedures, American students will be better prepared to serve as productive members of the global community.

3

......

CHILDREN CONSTRUCTING KNOWLEDGE

*T*he raucous sound of irate chicks almost drowned out the voice of first-grade teacher Chris Valentine as she gathered twenty-three children around her. Eight posters, labeled Squeaker, Chirp-Chirp, Peep, Feathers, Stripey, Chicago Jackson, Alex, Jr., and Kate, hung beside her chair, displaying data the students were keeping on their noisy classroom pets. The chicks were now nine days old and ready for their second weigh-in, but the children were told that before they updated their chicks statistics, they should estimate what they thought the weight would be.

Nicole collected Feathers, her data sheet, a pan balance, and a box of unifix cubes to use as units of measurement. Her friend Tanya came over to help her get started.

First they estimated. Taking note of the fact that just six days earlier Feathers had weighed nine cubes, Nicole estimated that her chick would now weigh ten cubes. But Tanya, commenting on how big Feathers had grown, estimated thirteen cubes.

Feathers was deftly placed in a deep plastic tub on one side of the pan balance scale and an identical tub was counterbalanced on the other side to hold the unifix cubes. The girls began their work. Nicole counted aloud as Tanya dropped cubes into the tub by twos. "Two . . . four . . . six . . . eight . . . now put in two more . . . ten," directed Nicole. The scale did not shift. "Maybe it has to be thirteen," said Nicole, conceding that perhaps Tanya's estimate was right. "Put in three more." The pan still did not balance. Nicole and Tanya exchanged looks of surprise. "Maybe get three more."

Tanya left to join another group, so Nicole continued alone. She began adding more cubes to the tub, one or two at a time, but did not count aloud. Finally, Feathers' tub began to rise. Nicole added just one more cube and Feathers' tub rose higher than the tub of cubes. Nicole reached in and removed several cubes, slowly replacing them one at a time until, once again, Feathers' tub sat too high.

Nicole reached in and removed one red cube. Feathers' tub sank slightly below the other and Nicole immediately replaced the cube, restoring the tub to its higher position. She carefully pulled out a green cube, with the same result. She repeated this action several more times, each time being careful to remove a different color cube and then returning it to the tub. But the pans never balanced. Finally, she shrugged her shoulders and counted the cubes in the tub.

"How many cubes?" asked Ms. Valentine.

"Twenty-three," she replied, "but I don't believe it."

"Why not?"

"She [Feathers] was only nine [Feathers' previous weight]. That's too much."

A boy from the next table stopped by to ask how much Feathers weighed. "Twenty-three," said Nicole. "It's too many."

He looked quizzically at Nicole. "The other ones are only like twenty-one," he said and returned to his own chick.

Nicole decided to weigh Feathers again, quickly dropping cubes into the bucket. This time she wasted little time trying to get the scale to balance, stopping when the pans sat almost level. Removing cubes by twos, she counted them into a pile.

"How many did you get this time?" asked her teacher.

"Twenty-three."

"Do you believe it?"

"Yeah, okay, I believe it," she said with a shrug and recorded the number next to her original estimate.

It was, indeed, hard to believe. Feathers had been the smallest chick at birth, and weighed a mere nine cubes when three days old. As the weights of her siblings were recorded and posted, word spread through the class that, at twenty-three cubes, Feathers was now the heaviest of the lot.

Nicole is experiencing math. She is acting on objects and noticing their relationships. She observes, tests, and retests. She uses her intuition and background knowledge to develop hypotheses, devise plans, draw conclusions. She communicates ideas. In essence, Nicole is constructing her own mathematical knowledge.

Children are curious by nature. They are born problem solvers. From the earliest age, they delight in their interactions with the world around them, handling, manipulating, experimenting. Most important, they take note of the physical changes and social responses brought on by their actions. And with each new encounter, they modify their perceptions of the world and begin to construct their own knowledge of the elements within their environment.

Similarly, a child's ability to learn the abstract processes and concepts integral to mathematics benefits from the opportunity to interact directly with the environment. As children manipulate objects, observe changes, develop trial-and-error methods of interaction, and reflect upon their experiences, they gradually construct their own understanding of the relationships between objects and concepts. By placing children in controlled, problem-solving situations and providing a supportive environment to communicate ideas, teachers can build effective learning opportunities.

Traditional approaches to mathematics usually focus on rote learning and prescribed algorithms. All students are expected to work toward the same objective, at the same time, in the same manner. For example, lessons are often designed to transmit a single method of computation through teacher demonstration and student repitition and practice. Advocates of this teaching model expect learners to absorb this method, commit it to memory, and recall it whenever it is needed. More focus is on the answer than on the thinking.

The NCTM standards recognize the experience and background knowledge that each child brings with them when they enter school. In order for children to make sense of the mathematics they are learning, they must construct for themselves personal understandings of the concepts and processes, using that background knowledge. Each student is seen as a unique individual who, given a meaningful situation and setting, is able to wrestle with a problem and devise a method to solve it. The focus is on the process—building an understanding that can be transferred to other situations.

CONSTRUCTING MEANINGS

Nicole and the other first graders in Ms. Valentine's class are used to tackling meaningful math problems. This time it was real chicks, real scales, real units of weight, and real jobs—reading, estimating, measuring, recording, and comparing. The procedure could have been accomplished more quickly and efficiently as a demonstration by Ms. Valentine, perhaps with a few students in front of the class, but as Ms. Valentine realizes, constructing knowledge is not a vicarious process.

Feathers weighed twenty-three cubes (or, as Nicole came close to discovering, more likely twenty-two and one-half cubes). But the weight of any one chick on a given day was not what was significant about the exercise. What was significant that day were the *processes* involved in discovering Feathers' weight and the relationship among the various elements of the lesson.

Closer analysis of Nicole at work shows a child actively involved in learning. Nicole's simple counting reveals a rudimentary understanding of addition. She added cubes by twos until she had reached her estimate of ten cubes. "Two, four, six, eight . . . now put in two more . . . ten," she said as her friend dropped cubes in by twos. "Put in three more," she added, so they'd reach Tanya's estimate of thirteen. Without realizing it, she was using the basic concept of missing addend subtraction.

When the scale failed to balance, Nicole became concerned with the weight of the individual cubes. She was determined to balance the scale, and when adding and removing single cubes did not help the pans balance, she decided to focus on their one apparent difference—color. Soon she discovered that this attribute was insignificant to her task. The second time Nicole weighed the chick, she ignored color differences, and quickly decided for herself when the tubs were "close enough," a concept basic to understanding measurement.

Nicole's original hypothesis, that Feathers would weigh only ten cubes, fell far short of Feathers' actual weight. Just how far short was hard to believe. Seeing the pile of twenty-three cubes in the tub hardly convinced her, and when she heard that the other chicks were weighing in lighter than little Feathers, she decided she'd better repeat the process.

This very sophisticated move for a first grader indicated her grasp of the multiple elements involved in the chicks as a group, and Feathers' assumed place within that group. The numbers did not make sense to her, so she repeated the process, this time more quickly and efficiently than the first. The results were the same, the evidence was hard to dispute. Twenty-three cubes. "Yeah, okay, I believe it," she conceded, and in the group discussion that followed, it was obvious that the others did as well.

Would Nicole have believed Feathers' weight if she had not been so actively involved in the process? Perhaps. But more important was the confidence and autonomy she exhibited in developing a process for measurement and evaluation. She made an initial prediction that reflected earlier findings. She tested several methods to get the pans of the scale level, but rather than abandoning the project when she failed to achieve the desired balance, decided for herself when the balance was "close enough." She knew when to

CHILDREN CONSTRUCTING KNOWLEDGE

question her results, and had enough confidence in herself to retest an answer that seemed unacceptable. Finally, she was able to accept that evidence as plausible and move on to the second phase of the day's lesson.

After all the groups had recorded their data and rehung their posters, the children reassembled around their teacher. It was time to discuss what they had discovered about the weights of their chicks. Ms. Valentine began by posing several questions, to which students actively responded. "How did you decide on your chick's estimated weight?" "Was your estimate more than or less than what your chick weighed?" "Which chick weighs the most?" "What did you notice about Feathers' weight from when she was born until now?"

After the group had talked about her questions, Ms. Valentine opened the discussion to student-initiated comment, allowing the children the freedom to discuss their own ideas about the chicks. Together, they analyzed the data, comparing the weights of the chicks.

Soon Ms. Valentine sent the students back to their seats. "Put everything away except for your unifix cubes," she instructed them. "And look toward the overhead."

The children quickly cleared their desks and turned toward the overhead screen. "Now, we know that Peep weighs twenty-one cubes and Chirp-Chirp weighs twenty cubes," Ms. Valentine began. "If we put Peep and Chirp-Chirp together on a scale, how much would they weigh?" She wrote the addition problem on the overhead:

$$21 + 20 = \underline{\qquad}$$

and told the children they could use cubes or any other props they needed to help them find a solution.

The hum of activity began immediately as Ms. Valentine moved about the room. Several children sat back confidently, explaining to Ms. Valentine how they had mentally computed the problem. Others worked singly or in pairs, using their unifix cubes to work out the answer. After about five minutes, Ms. Valentine returned to the front of the class and called on students to share their methods.

Nicole and Tanya had worked together with the unifix cubes. They quickly went to the overhead and began arranging transparent tiles to represent the cubes. "Tanya is making twenty-one and I'm making twenty," explained Nicole as they strung out two long lines of cubes. "We each got our number," continued Tanya. "This is Chirp-Chirp," she said, pointing to the line of twenty squares. "And this is Peep." She pointed to the line of twenty-one. "We know that 20 and 20 is 40 and we added one more."

"Danielle, you used the cubes but you grouped them differently," said Ms. Valentine beckoning Danielle to the front of the class. "Watch how Danielle

groups them." Danielle began to set her tiles in double sets of five.

Soon Danielle was ready to explain her method, but as she pointed to each row of five, she recited, "ten . . . twenty . . . thirty." She stopped, noticing something was wrong. Slowly, she began to remove some tiles. She appeared confused.

Ms. Valentine told her to take a few minutes to figure out what she'd done, and used the time to let the children who'd used mental math share their reasoning. "I knew that 2 plus 2 was 4. I knew that 1 plus 0 was 1," began Albert. "So it just makes 41 because the two 10s and two 10s equal 40 and 1 plus 0 equals 1. So it's 41."

By the time several others had shared, Danielle was ready to continue. She had replaced all of the original squares and pointed to the rows of markers as she quickly counted, "five, ten, fifteen, twenty, twenty-five, thirty, thirty-five, forty, and one is forty-one."

MAKING CONNECTIONS

Hands-on activity takes on new meaning when the hands are needed to gently move, measure, and manage a squawking, flapping chick. Ms. Valentine's first graders directly experienced the physical attributes of shape, weight, and balance while collecting their data. The activity itself provided the motivation to learn, and the fact that Nicole and her classmates could discover something totally unexpected significantly enhanced the thrill of discovery. But understanding is not built solely by experience. Experience and discovery must be accompanied by children *making connections* between previously internalized concepts and newly developed interpretations of the world.

The activity of weighing chicks set the stage for discussion that was essential to the work that followed. The discussion allowed the children to take ownership of their experience by giving structure and meaning to arbitrary numbers and new concepts. Combining the weights of Peep and Chirp-Chirp provided a logical reason to add

CHILDREN CONSTRUCTING KNOWLEDGE

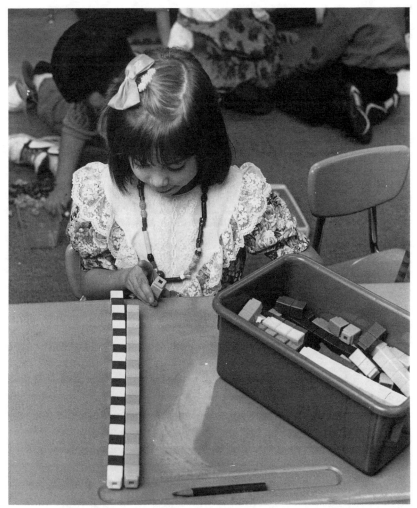

Using manipulatives helps young children make sense of abstract ideas and processes.

double-digit numbers and gave significance to the numerals. The children knew what they were adding, for they had each handled and counted twenty or twenty-one blocks just minutes before. Writing the numbers horizontally encouraged the children to think about them as twenty-one and twenty, not just as a two followed by a one and another two followed by a zero. A vertical arrangement might have made a digit-by-digit view more likely.

Prior to this lesson, Ms. Valentine's class had had multiple experiences with place value and double-digit addition, and the children were well prepared to solve this problem. The children showed a full range of sophistication in their various solutions. Many children tackled the numbers quickly, without the aid of any manipulatives; but those who were not ready to perform the addition mentally had the time and props to establish a solution, and a partner with whom they could share the task and co-invent a plan of action.

VALUABLE DISCOURSE

The lesson culminated when the children explained their solutions to their classmates. Albert quickly and easily verbalized the procedure he used to add the two numbers. Nicole and Tanya jointly shared the responsibility for explaining a method in which they assigned a row of cubes to represent each chick's weight. Danielle, who had used an elaborate grouping procedure, started her explanation easily enough, but soon got tangled up explaining her less familiar method. Ms. Valentine wisely allowed Danielle the time she needed to think through her work and she was soon able to explain her steps in a logical manner.

Verbalizing a thought process focuses ideas for a student. It organizes thinking. It solidifies concepts and processes and establishes them as a basis for future reference. And it provides ownership of ideas.

Often, children solve a problem intuitively and are unable to state how or why they gave a particular answer. The initial solution may have come to them in such a flash of insight that they did not even see their own procedure. It is only when they explain how they arrived at a solution that they actually develop and establish their procedure and build processes to use and modify when faced with similar problems.

When children explain their thinking, they have the opportunity to decide for themselves whether or not they are correct. The process of explanation enables them to revisit their thinking and say, "Yes, I'm right. I've explained it, I know this makes sense. I've confirmed what I thought." If their response is flawed, they can stop themselves and say, "This is not making sense, let me retrace my steps and decide where I went wrong. Then I can figure this out."

Ms. Valentine's class is a terrific example of students gaining math power. Knowing that each child must actively construct his own knowledge, this skilled teacher has provided the students with meaningful situations, asked questions that cause students to think about their activity and the mathematics, and then provided them the time to reflect on their experiences and thought processes. Discourse is integral to her curriculum—children are provided with multiple opportunities to share, debate, explain, and evaluate their ideas in small- and large-group settings. When student discourse is encouraged and vital to the learning process, students begin to accept responsibility for their learning rather than feel the responsibility belongs to the teacher.

It is interesting to note that Ms. Valentine's class is very diverse. Some children have been identified by the school system as "gifted and talented," and a significant number have special academic and social needs. A range of culture and ethnicity is represented in the classroom. Yet every child participates in and benefits from the math lessons.

Recognizing that children (and adults) need to construct their own understanding helps teachers to reach the full range of students. Traditional methods of direct instruction, while appearing to work for some, fail to work for a large percentage of students. Those who benefit little from traditional approaches include children from all achievement groups—from average students to those in special education, both those considered "slow learners" and those labeled "gifted and talented."

All children are unique. They enter learning situations with different backgrounds. They exhibit distinctive learning styles. They develop in their own way and at their own pace. Consequently, each child will interpret and connect ideas differently and must construct for himself or herself the connections and relationships among those concepts essential to understanding mathematics.

4

· · · · · ·

TEACHERS AS PROBLEM SOLVERS

Sue Evans, a first-grade teacher, is committed to allowing her students to construct their own mathematical understanding. She admits, though, that even after participating for two years in a program designed to help teachers understand and use the kinds of ideas found in the NCTM standards publications, she still must fight the urge to intervene. She likes to recount one classroom experience that illustrates how children can be trusted to solve complex problems for themselves when provided with meaningful situations—sometimes going far beyond typical first-grade problems.

"It was near the end of the school year and we were doing fractions and I was having the kids dividing different objects into parts with masking tape," she relates. "The children got to choose the object they wanted to divide and then draw a number from a pile. This number told them how many parts they were to create. One group of three average-achieving girls chose to divide the 'cubbies,' an area of thirty-two separate boxes stacked sixteen on top of sixteen. The number they drew was six.

"One-sixth of thirty-two! Well, that was one of my most difficult problems of the day, certainly more difficult than any I'd envisioned when planning this activity. When I saw the task ahead of them I thought, 'They'll never be able to do this.' But they wanted to try. So I went over to them and started asking a series of questions, trying to sway them to do it my way. But they wouldn't hear of it, saying, 'No, no, we've got our own ideas,' so I went to other children.

"From time to time I would look over toward the cubbies and notice that things looked confused. They had tape all over. When it came to their turn to talk about what they'd done, I thought, 'I'll skip them, maybe they won't notice.' But no, they had to explain. I thought, 'Oh, those poor girls, they're not going to be able to explain this.'

"Then one of the girls said, 'One-sixth of thirty-two cubbies is five and one-third.' All I could say was, 'What?' and she said it again. 'One-sixth of thirty-two cubbies is five and one-third.' And I said, 'Can you explain that?'

"The girls explained how they took the cubbies and divided them into six parts and they had five cubbies in each part. They had two cubbies left over, so they took those two cubbies and divided each one into thirds, so that would be six. Then they went back and counted and it was five and one-third.

"Well, I was just shocked with what they were doing! If you wrote on a piece of paper one-sixth of thirty-two, it would seem an impossible task for first graders. But the cubbies were there, they had the tape, they could count, they could change it around."

Certainly, the performance of these first graders would surprise most adults, and indeed, few children in traditional classrooms would be able to solve a problem such as one-sixth of thirty-two. But given real-world situations, ones in which they are truly interested, children often attempt, and realize, fantastic results.

Research (see, for example, Whitin et al. 1990 and Carpenter and Moser 1983) suggests that children enter school able to solve real problems that require mathematics skills they have not yet been taught. But sadly, by the time they reach second grade, many of these same students exhibit a decrease in the types of creative abilities that assist problem solving.

Why is there deterioration in problem-solving success? One explanation appears to be an emphasis on "teaching" isolated algorithms, rules based on rote memorization, rather than letting young children construct their own understanding. This leaves children little to fall back on when faced with new situations. Rather than think through the problem, they look for a rule that they have been taught—often to no avail. Problem solving in the real world is not based on memorized performance. It requires thinking. Like the girls in Ms. Evans' class, children need to tackle problems with confidence, understanding, creativity, and perseverance.

One student, who appeared to be mathematically advanced while in second grade, became lost when he moved on to third. Knowing that children often confuse left and right, his second grade teacher had told her students that when adding and subtracting double-digit numbers, they should always start on the side toward the windows. This child, and probably some others, interpreted this literally as the rule to be followed. Unfortunately for him, the windows were on the other side of the room when he got to third grade. While this scenario demonstrates an extreme misuse of "rules," is it that far removed from having children learn "borrowing" and "carrying" without understanding place value, or having them rely on "clue words" embedded in a story problem when deciding on a course of action?

As problem solvers themselves, teachers need to learn how their students are thinking about the mathematics and then use that information to plan instruction. Understanding the meaning of mathematical symbols is critical to success in mathematics. It can also be an indicator of a student's depth of understanding of the mathematics.

Studies (Carpenter et al. 1997) indicate that elementary students can solve story problems more easily than problems without context. Allowing students to solve these types of problems provides teachers with insight into how well their students understand the "is equal to" symbol (see Figure 4–1). As students build understanding of computation through story contexts, they need to record their work using symbols to represent the elements of the stories. That way, symbols begin to take on meanings that can be transferred to mathematics problems with no context.

How can teachers regularly create an atmosphere that encourages growth of mathematical thinking skills? Like Sue Evans, many approach the teaching of mathematics with the same tenacity and creativity with which they wish their students to approach the task of learning mathematics. They view the teaching of mathematics as a problem-solving activity in and of itself—an effort to find situations and problems for children that will enable them to make sense of the mathematical aspects of the world in which they live and work, as well as to make sense of the symbols that are used to communicate about mathematics.

Teachers are responsible for controlling the classroom setting. To incorporate the NCTM standards, they must present problems and provide situations that enable students to construct their understanding of the math. They need to build on these situations by asking questions and guiding discussions so that their students will construct understanding while staying close to the main mathematics goals of the curriculum.

An essential role of the teacher, then, is to look for evidence of her students' mathematical understanding, find situations that will be meaningful or interesting to children, and then develop math content from these situations. Conversely, she must also take mathematically relevant concepts and create interesting learning experiences that

Figure 4–1
DIAGNOSTIC ACTIVITY TO DETERMINE STUDENTS'
DEVELOPMENT OF CONCEPTS OF EQUALITY

Overview
The "is equal to" symbol (=) is used in many textbooks as though its meaning is self-evident. Children are given few opportunities to build a conceptual understanding of the symbol. In fact, many children in first through sixth grades interpret the symbol as though it means "now find the answer" (Falkner et al. 1999).

Level
Multiple levels of difficulty, first through sixth grade

Procedure
1. Create several relatively simple problems such as the following:
    I. Level 1 (approximately first grade)
        $8 = 3 + 5$ Is this true? Yes ____ No ____ Tell why or why not.
    II. Level 2 (approximately second, third, or fourth grade)
        ____ $= 17 - 8$ What number goes in the blank to make the number sentence true? Explain how you got your answer.
    III.Level 3 (approximately second through sixth grades)
        $5 + 9 =$ ____ $+ 8$ What number goes in the blank to make the number sentence true? Explain how you got your answer.

2. Before reviewing the problems with the students, have them solve the following problems. If necessary, read the problems aloud to make sure all students understand the questions.
    I. Level 1
        Angie gave 8 stickers to Bruce. Now Angie has 5 stickers. How many stickers did Angie have to start with?
    II. Level 2
        Destiny had 17 stickers. She gave 8 to Denise. How many stickers does Destiny have now?
    III.Level 3
        Destiny had 5 stickers. Her mom gave her 9 more. Angie had 8 stickers. Her mom gave her some more. Now she has as many stickers as Destiny. How many stickers did her mom give her?

Analysis
Problems such as those in the first group indicate whether a student has a narrow concept of equality. When adding the story problems that match the equations, determine whether the students solve the story problems more or less successfully than the numeric equations.

Extensions
In order to broaden students' understanding, offer activities that present the concept of equality in a variety of ways. For example, use the equality sign in different contexts and situations as you teach. Let students see that its correct message is one of equal value for the numbers it separates, rather than telling them to solve for an answer.

will make these concepts meaningful to students, again based on her observations. This is a teacher's problem to solve. Teachers can call upon a variety of sources for ideas and guidance, including personal experience, school district instructional guides, and documents such as the NCTM standards.

Problem-solving situations lead children to develop their own ideas and understandings through direct experience and discourse. In day-to-day classroom situations, a variety of ways exist to encourage and support students as they develop their mathematical understanding. Sometimes, a teacher can direct children toward the intended outcome through careful questioning or guided class discussion. At other times, it may be necessary for the teacher to establish a stronger foundation of more rudimentary concepts.

The students in Marina Lopez's second-grade class were beginning to work on subtraction of double-digit numbers. Ms. Lopez knows the importance of making sure students understand place value and is aware of young children's difficulty with "regrouping" situations. She believes that it is important to begin with regrouping problems; otherwise, children tend to ignore the numbers' place value.

Ms. Marina Lopez wrote the problem "43 – 35" on the board. The children made several attempts to solve the problem and were soon frustrated. Some had subtracted the smaller digit from the larger one. Others had tried to start with the tens and didn't know what to do next. And some had actually determined the correct answer, but did not realize it or understand that it was correct. It wasn't long before many of the children declared, "That's too hard. We don't know how."

Since it was close to the end of the class, Ms. Lopez debated what to do. Certainly, one of her options was to show the traditional procedure for getting an answer, but after a moment's thought, Ms. Lopez decided not to continue. "Okay," she said to the children, "if you think it's too hard, let's think about it some more and we'll come back to it another time."

That night, Ms. Lopez went home and thought about real-world situations that would lead her students to solve the problem. Knowing that the children had been busy planning a student-operated "Fun Fair," she seized on an authentic situation for them to work out.

The next morning Ms. Lopez reminded her students that in listing the supplies they would need to operate all their games, they had determined they needed a total of twenty-four beanbags. Good news, she continued. She had come across sixteen beanbags in the school storage closet. How many more beanbags, she asked, would they need? Vitally interested in the answer, the children found it quickly and fairly easily.

"How did you solve this?" she asked.

"I knew that 6 plus 8 is 14," said one, "and 16 plus 8 must be 24. So the answer had to be 8."

"I used my fingers to count 17, 18, 19, 20, 21, 22, 23, 24," said another as she tapped each finger in turn. "Then I counted the fingers."

"I subtracted 16 from 24," said Della, who had paper and pencil in hand. She went on to explain her procedure—just the direction in which Ms. Lopez wanted to move the class.

Discussing the various methods that they had used—thinking of it as addition with a missing addend, counting on, and a paper-and-pencil subtraction procedure—the class began to notice how the ideas were alike and different. As the children's ideas continued, Ms. Lopez recorded some of the methods using numbers and symbols. She then brought back the problem of the previous day. The children attacked the problem with new confidence and solved it easily. One said, "It's just the same as with the beanbags!" Most children chose one of the procedures shared by their classmates, but some invented new ways to solve the problem. Ms. Lopez again had the children talk about how the methods were alike and different. As the lesson closed, Ms. Lopez thought, "Tomorrow I'll give them a story problem using 54 – 37 and I'll challenge them to see if everyone can try Della's way or one of the other subtraction procedures that didn't involve counting."

Ms. Lopez saw the need for the children to establish stronger connections between concrete experience and a computational exercise presented in symbols. But it took flexibility and self-confidence on her part to stop her planned lesson when she saw her students were not ready. There is a fine balance between the needs of children and the demands of the curriculum or textbook. Feeling the pressure to move through the curriculum as scheduled, many teachers might not have chosen to invest the extra time in what seems a simple subtraction process. However, just as students need time to think when solving problems, teachers must find their own solutions to teaching and learning problems.

The need for children to construct strong mathematical foundations is too important to warrant their teachers pushing them ahead merely for the sake of completing a unit, and educators like Ms. Lopez feel that time spent ensuring that their students fully understand the rudimentary concepts is never wasted. Although such an approach may take more time initially, extra time spent in the early stages of learning will be rewarded later. Students who construct their own procedures are much better positioned to transfer their knowledge to new circumstances, everyday problems, and the mathematics concepts they will study in the future. And teachers are likely to find that the need for reteaching is minimized because there is much less forgetting.

The ultimate goal, then, must not be to "get through" the lesson, the unit, or the year. Rather, the goal must be to construct a solid foundation while children are in the primary grades, so that they can get through the more complex problems that they will encounter in later grades. To this end, a long-term teaching plan, whether teacher-developed or based on a text, should be used with flexibility, insight, understanding, and continual reevaluation.

As teachers place themselves in the role of problem solver and see solutions that will help children build a clearer understanding of mathematics, they can develop effective classroom instructional programs for mathematics. For those who believe that children benefit most when they construct their own understanding of mathematics, the focus while planning teaching must be on valuing the same kinds of problem-solving processes that are often used in solving mathematics problems.

One way to approach the process of *teaching* mathematics is to view it as analogous to the process of *doing* mathematics. Even in the most challenging situations, mathematicians often follow a simple, four-step problem-solving process. The plan, which allows them to understand, compute, and revise (if necessary), enables them to solve most problems they encounter. The plan requires that they:

1. understand the problem
2. develop a plan that they feel will solve the problem
3. try the plan to see if it works
4. look at the results to see if they make sense for that problem. If the results do not make sense, they move back to the first step of the process and begin again.

In teaching, a similar four-step process can be used. In this process teachers must first understand the mathematics that is to be taught and the children who are learning the mathematics. The second step is to develop a plan that reflects that understanding. The third step is to provide classroom instruction that implements the plan. And the fourth step is to evaluate students' success, reflect back, and possibly revise the approach.

This is one method of establishing classroom practices that respect child development, ensure the application of sound educational principles, and accommodate the needs of individual classrooms, teachers, and children. However, those classrooms in which teachers incorporate this process and develop instructional programs that reflect the recommendations found in the NCTM standards will share many of the following characteristics. They will:

- focus on the process of mathematics as much as on right answers;
- encourage students to describe their thinking orally and in writing;
- reflect on students' thinking and use it to plan instruction that moves students forward in their mathematical understanding and skill;
- encourage students to be less reliant on the teacher and better able to validate their own answers as correct;
- encourage students to be persistent and willing to seek alternative ways to solve difficult problems;
- demonstrate, model, and accept mathematical ideas in a variety of ways. This will include multicultural uses of mathematics as well as hands-on experiences that use a variety of materials;
- help students to see that mathematics is a useful and interesting area of learning;
- enable children to become problem solvers and users of mathematics in their everyday lives;
- develop an efficient and encompassing program of mathematics instruction;
- have a flexible plan, designed to meet the needs of children while maintaining focus on long-range instructional goals.

Teachers like Chris Valentine, Sue Evans, and Marina Lopez are focused on the "big ideas" of mathematics. They do not rely on textbooks that break mathematics down into isolated steps, a practice that fails to help children make sense of the content and processes they are encountering. Children need to make connections among interrelated concepts in order to develop a deeper conceptual understanding of mathematics. Evidence suggests that a piecemeal approach to teaching mathematics does not effectively help children grow in their mathematical thinking and skill, and does not help them learn to solve real problems (Greeno 1991). Teachers who listen to children's conversations about, and explanations of, mathematics procedures encountered throughout the school day and who observe how their students approach problem-solving situations are engaging in the kind of thoughtful practice that drives effective teaching. As they collect data on the students' understandings and misunderstandings; document this evidence; look for patterns of skills, behavior, and engagement; and use this information to guide planning and integrate activities, discourse, texts, and other resources, they will be better able to help children focus on and learn the important ideas of mathematics.

5

......

BUILDING UNDERSTANDING

Martin Lee, the teacher's assistant for the kindergarten, asked Sara to count for him. She happily and confidently complied, counting to thirty-five with no hesitation. Then Mr. Lee showed Sara seventeen dried beans. "Count these for me, Sara, and tell me how many there are."

Sara smiled broadly and counted away, "One, two, three . . ." However, she had no way of keeping track of which beans had been counted. Some beans were counted several times, others not at all. After a while, Sara announced, "Twenty-four." She was done.

Mr. Lee was trying to find out what Sara understood about numbers and counting. Based on his knowledge of how children gradually develop concepts of counting, he may not have been surprised that Sara was not yet able to connect her rote counting skills to the concept of one-to-one correspondence using real objects. Sara had no organized, or rational, way of counting a group of real objects.

Many kindergartners are able to rote count when they come to school. This does not mean that they understand what they are doing, even though they have given a "right" answer. When teachers understand at what level a child is being successful, they can make informed decisions about appropriate next steps for a student's instructional plan.

In this case, Mr. Lee knew that kindergarten children should begin to demonstrate an understanding of the counting process. This means that they can keep track of their count, count each object just once, assign only one counting number to each object, and associate the last number that they count with the number of objects in the group rather than thinking of it as the name of the last object counted. Children like Sara, who despite their ability to rote count cannot make such con-

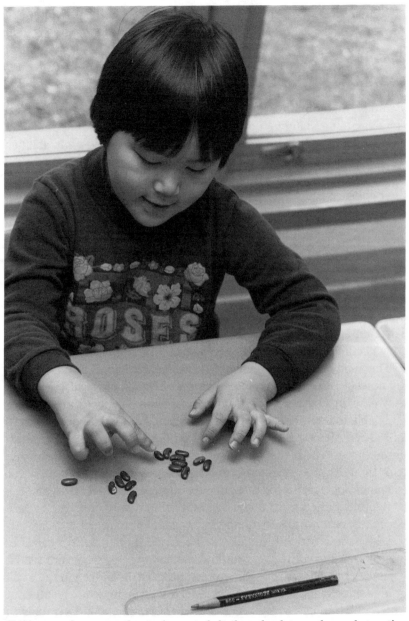

Children need many math experiences to help them develop number and operation sense.

THINKING LIKE MATHEMATICIANS

nections, need experiences that will develop these concepts. Advancing Sara too quickly, based only on her counting skills, would be a mistake.

UNDERSTANDING HOW CHILDREN LEARN

The best mathematics programs are built on three types of understanding: understanding how children learn; understanding the mathematics itself; and understanding the background, needs, and abilities of each student.

Learning is an active process. From birth, children interact with their physical and social environments to build a framework of knowledge, a mental organization that then becomes the foundation for making sense of future events. New situations and perceptions are assimilated into this existing scheme of knowledge, but often they do not fit into the child's current notions about the world. Consequently, the child must modify and adapt what she already knows to accommodate this new information. In this way, the child constructs new knowledge and understanding to be used in future situations. Through assimilation and accommodation, children are continually constructing knowledge. They are learning.

The ability of young children to reason abstractly is limited; learning must be directly linked to personal actions and physical objects. As they pass through the early stages of childhood, children are increasingly able to apply representational language and symbols to objects and ideas. Moving into the primary grades—kindergarten through grade three—children's modes of reasoning expand and more complex thought processes emerge, broadening the opportunities for learning. But even for the most mature students, mental activity is supported most effectively when it is well grounded in concrete experiences and real-world situations that are familiar to them.

Like Sara, most children like to listen and imitate, and because of their increasing vocabulary and their ability to remember and repeat what they have heard, it is difficult to judge what children in the early grades actually know and understand. Being sensitive to the stages at which children can apply representational language and symbols to ideas, understanding the development of their reasoning ability, and realizing the link between concrete experience and abstract thought are fundamental to mathematics instruction.

To understand concepts, to truly *learn*, a child must be confronted with problems that are challenging—problems that cannot be solved by routine repetition of previously learned procedures. Such problems will be most valued by the student when they are presented in meaningful situations that relate to the child's background. This provides a "hook" to associate new experiences with old so that preexisting notions can be modified and conceptual understanding constructed.

While more mature learners can represent objects mentally, for most young children, reasoning and perceptions are limited to direct personal experience; they require physical action and manipulation of objects. Obviously, the greater the variety of activities and the wider the assortment of materials, the richer will be their learning experiences and the stronger their foundation of understanding. However, it must be noted that learning experiences are not solely comprised of physical activity. The adaptation of mental structure necessary for learning to take place requires adequate opportunity to reflect on an event.

Somewhat paradoxically, independent construction of knowledge is often facilitated by social interaction. Children need to reflect on their physical actions to build understanding; but verbalizing their ideas helps them to organize their thoughts and reorder their thinking. Exchanging mathematical notions with classmates and adults helps to clarify problems, provides insight into alternative solution strategies, and identifies potential conflicts or misconceptions. Communicating so that other students understand a solution requires a child to focus on descriptions, define procedures, and rationalize conclusions. Conversely, listening to others provides new perceptions and encourages students to further modify and reorganize their own ideas.

Arleen Cohen-Hart likes to provide many opportunities for her third graders to explain their thinking. One of the class's favorites is a mental math game in which students must quickly choose a problem, solve it mentally, and then explain how they arrived at their solution (see Figure 5–1). By offering a range of difficulty, Ms. Cohen-Hart accommodates the mathematical range of the students; by limiting the number of displayed problems, she ensures that each problem will be explained several ways. Ms. Cohen-Hart notes that almost every time she uses this activity, the students' reactions indicate that they have heard strategies that they would not have thought of on their own and that they are anxious to try.

UNDERSTANDING THE MATHEMATICS

Before teachers can plan or implement a program that reflects the NCTM standards, they should understand what "knowledge of

Figure 5–1
MENTAL MATH ACTIVITY

Overview
Have children do arithmetic mentally and explain their thinking.

Level
Adaptable

Grouping
Whole class or small group

Materials
- Overhead projector
- Transparencies with five to ten mixed computation problems appropriate for the class.

     A wide range of difficulty helps ensure that each student will be able to participate in the activity. Here are some sample problems for levels one through four:

Level 1	*Level 2*	*Level 3*	*Level 4*
2 + 2 + 2	35 – 21	68 – 39	8 x 12
2 + 2 + 3	42 – 14	8 x 9	195 + 308
3 + 3 + 10	53 – 6	80 x 9	15 x 23
7 + 8	53 – 16	35 – 21	67 + 84
14 + 8	53 – 36	67 + 84	179 x 9
14 + 18	43 + 88	62 + 49	102 x 98

Procedure
- Have students pair up.
- Before turning on the overhead, tell students that when they see the problems on the screen, they are to choose two or three problems and work them out in their minds.
- Suggest the possibility of choosing two or three problems that relate to one another if they see them.
- Ask students to be ready to share their answers with their partners and be able to explain how they arrived at their solution.
- Turn on the overhead projector. Have students signal when they are ready to share.
- When all students have signaled that they are ready, have partners share their answers and solutions with each other.
- Have students come together as a class. Each time a child shares a solution and method of deriving that solution, ask if anyone did that example in a different way. Discuss different methods for finding solutions.

Extensions
- During whole-group discussion, have students try to explain their partner's approach if it was different from their own.
- Have student pairs make up their own problems for the activity. For each problem they create, they should write out at least one method for solving it.

mathematics" means and have some level of comfort with the many concepts integral to mathematics. Then they need to understand how to present these concepts in a developmentally appropriate manner.

This does not mean that every elementary teacher must have the mathematics background of a secondary mathematics teacher. It does mean that they should "think like mathematicians," just as they want their students to do. It means that teachers must recognize mathematics not as a static collection of "right answers," but as a dynamic activity in which people (including children and teachers) make personal sense out of quantities, shapes, sizes, and patterns.

Teachers should have familiarity with the "big ideas" of the mathematics, not just at one grade level, but across at least several grades. A teacher's instructional focus may be on the grade level at which she works, but having some level of knowledge about previous and later grades is essential for differentiating instruction to meet the needs of a diverse community of learners. Teaching and learning mathematics can be a reciprocally beneficial activity between teachers and students.

Children learn through observation and social interaction with the external world. Because understanding mathematics also requires that specific observed relationships be generalized and represented symbolically, mathematical understanding is built by reasoning, an internal process that is recognized by one of the NCTM process standards.

Observable characteristics, such as size, weight, color, and shape, provide knowledge about physical attributes. Words and names provide a common nomenclature with which to communicate. A child building with a set of blocks soon discovers their physical properties: edges and corners keep blocks from rolling, larger blocks balance better at the bottom than at the top of a stack, and blocks hurt when they land on a toe. The terms *rectangle*, *tower*, and *heavy* provide the social context with which the child can communicate about her blocks and her discoveries. But it is an understanding about the relationships among, and numerical ideas about, the blocks that provides the framework for mathematics. Which ones are bigger? What does *bigger* mean? Are there more red blocks than blue? How many more? How many different ways can these blocks be categorized?

Early mathematics knowledge is directly linked to physical knowledge. To see relationships, children must observe the nature of things. Such knowledge cannot be built without adequate opportunities to observe and act on objects, without sufficient time to reflect on the consequences of those actions, and without ample opportunity to communicate about these observations. Inherent in any good mathematics program are opportunities for children to construct relationships and make sense of numbers through classifying, comparing, ordering, counting, measuring, and patterning, along with opportunities to reconstruct their actions through reflection and discourse.

Upon careful examination, many seemingly simple mathematical concepts reveal multiple layers of complexity. Concepts that do not appear difficult on the surface may hold subtle challenges for young children and their teachers. Keeping in mind both the nature of the child and the nature of the math concept can alert teachers to potential instructional difficulties. Listening to children explain their thinking or looking at students' work and students *at* work can help teachers understand these subtle challenges, as well as provide the basis for next instructional steps.

One common example of a complex mathematics concept is that of fractions. Ms. Evans, the teacher discussed in Chapter 4, whose first-grade fraction unit includes many hands-on activities, is aware of the problems students can encounter when learning about fractions. She knows that at its most basic level, the concept of a fraction is relatively simple because it is so often experienced in everyday sharing situations; naming two equal parts as halves is experienced by most children many times in their daily lives. However, extending this rudimentary concept to a generalized understanding of fractions, especially one that incorporates the use of fraction *symbols*, is much more difficult.

Ms. Evans is familiar with the concepts integral to fractions and is prepared for the misconceptions and difficulties in generalizing that her students may develop along the way. Children expect fractions in symbolic form to act like the whole numbers with which they are just becoming comfortable. Young children often struggle with the illogical characteristics of fractions, not the least of which is the seemingly absurd notion that the value of a fraction decreases if the value of its denominator increases.

A child in first (or even second) grade is often still grappling with the symbolic representations of whole numbers. The number 1 represents one of something, 2 represents two. Next she learns that sometimes a 1 and 2 are placed side by side to form a different number, 12. It is difficult for the child who does not yet fully understand this combination to then accept that a 1 and a 2 written vertically with a small line between them is something else altogether, one-half. Sometimes the symbol is even written horizontally with a slanted line between the 1 and the 2, making interpretation even more challenging.

Generalization of the fraction concept is much more difficult than interpreting the symbol. "One-half" is easy when it is encountered in context, such as dividing an apple into two equal pieces for a snack. But extending that idea to one-third, one-fourth, one-fifth, and then to the idea that the denominator tells how many parts the whole is divided into and the numerator tells how many of the parts are used, is indeed difficult for most children. To further complicate the issue, the "whole" to which the denominator is applied can represent either a single object or an entire collection of objects.

Like Ms. Evans, teachers who have a basic understanding of both the mathematics concepts and how children approach those concepts are prepared with developmentally appropriate, yet mathematically logical, instructional approaches. Many decide it is better to delay extensive use of fraction symbols until the children are reasonably comfortable in their understanding of the symbolization of place value, which probably doesn't occur until the upper elementary grades.

Unfortunately, as desirable as it may be, delaying fraction symbols is usually overridden by local curricula, texts, or standardized tests. But Ms. Evans and her colleagues do their best to maintain a hands-on approach by regularly incorporating spoken or written fraction words into their discussions—"one-half of the class," "three-fourths of the orange." Their students are provided frequent, comprehensive, hands-on experiences, either in real-world situations or through the use of manipulative materials, to develop the part-whole concept. Furthermore, these teachers take into account the fact that such experiences are especially critical when the "whole" represents a collection of things rather than a single object.

Interestingly enough, manipulative materials, which are often helpful to students as they work with whole numbers, may not be nearly as helpful with fractions. Some studies have suggested that, because manipulative materials establish the whole for the student, they prevent the student from fully developing the concept of the whole for fractions (Empson 1995; Ball 1993). This phenomenon was effectively demonstrated to a group of teachers at a mathematics workshop. Each participant was given one red and two blue cubes. "What fraction of the set of cubes is red?" asked the facilitator. "One-third," everyone replied quickly. After telling them to keep that set, the facilitator gave each teacher two more cubes, this time one red and only one blue.

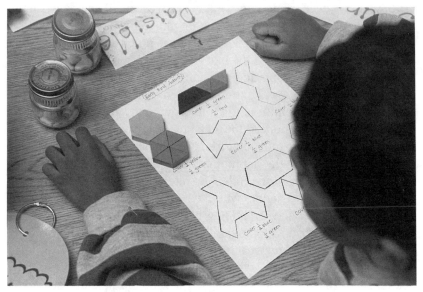

Young children, especially those who encounter fraction symbols in the early grades, need a variety of hands-on exeriences to help them develop the part-whole concept.

"Now what fraction of this set is red?" she asked. Once again, they all replied correctly, "One-half." Finally, the leader instructed the teachers to put the two sets together and said, "Now you have a set of five cubes. Two of them are red. Does this mean that one-third plus one-half equals two-fifths?" The teachers quickly recognized the misconception inherent in this demonstration. It's not easy to hold onto the whole in this situation, since there is no context. The original whole was the set of three objects and the one red cube represented one third of the set. Adding one-half to that one-third requires that the half is part of the same set, or whole, as the third.

Children as young as those in first grade can learn to create their own context for solving fraction problems by making drawings. Evidence suggests that when a student draws her own models for the whole, she makes a strong connection with that whole and can use it to build better concepts of the fractions (Empson 1995).

The importance of understanding the mathematics is not confined to overtly complex concepts like fractions. Even seemingly simple concepts such as those that underlie whole numbers can be complicated. For example, many children have difficulty understanding place value, but by being alert to the children's level of understanding and then using many hands-on activities and opportunities to share and discuss their activities, teachers can help them construct a deeper understanding of this concept.

This became clear to Arleen Cohen-Hart and her colleagues when they decided to conduct one-on-one mathematics interviews with the first-, second-, and third-grade students in their school. They discovered that, although the students were able to read and even to compute with double-digit numbers, many of the children did not fully understand place value.

In the assessment, each student was given a series of tasks involving the number 17. First the student was asked to read it, then to count out that many chips. Virtually all the children performed these tasks with ease. Then the teacher pointed to the numeral. Circling the 7 with her finger, she said, "Use these chips to show me how many this part of the numeral means." The near universal response in all three grades was correct—seven chips. Next, the teacher circled the 1 and said, "Now show me with the chips how many this part of the numeral means." Almost every first grader, a majority of the second graders, and many third graders responded by showing a single chip. Even after a follow-up query ("Yes it is a one, but does it mean anything different in *this* numeral?"), most of the children still said it meant just one chip. These students needed continuing opportunities to help them construct their understanding of place value.

Sometimes it helps when teachers put themselves in the place of the child. At an elementary math workshop, Ms. Cohen-Hart shared a video of Miko, a second-grade student who is having difficulty regrouping. Miko was asked to solve the problem 45 + 17 = _____. She rewrote the problem in vertical form and promptly wrote a 1 above the 4 in the tens column. Then she stopped. Asked by Ms. Cohen-Hart what she was thinking, Miko responded, "I know that 5 + 7 is 12 and that I have to 'carry the 1' over here [she pointed to the tens column], but I don't know what to do with the 11 I have left." When asked where she had heard the word *carry*, Miko explained that her father had told her. Miko was being frustrated by rules for which she had no understanding.

The teachers agreed that Miko's lack of place value understanding indicated that she might be solving computational problems by rote procedures that she did not fully understand. They discussed how teachers who are aware of the complexities of place value and the potential for common misconceptions among young children are better able to plan appropriate instructional strategies. These teachers use counting in ways that build place value concepts. They give children problems they can solve by using their background knowledge and invented procedures. Such invention encourages interpretation of numbers as whole quantities, rather than digit-by-digit procedures that ignore place value. They allow children to interrelate their work with materials and symbols for as long as necessary to more fully develop the notion that the one in the tens place means one ten, and not just one. It is unfortunate when children like Miko feel that they must resort to the magic of a memorized algorithm that makes no sense to them: "carry the one over here," or "knock on the door in the tens column and borrow a one." Dependence on rote memorization of rules can prove devastating in the later mathematical development of these children.

The teachers then went on to do an activity themselves using base-ten blocks to solve the same addition problem. First, they were asked to show 45. All of them did so by grouping four "longs," each of which represented ten units, and five ones. Then they were asked to use another set of blocks to show 17. Once again, each used one long to represent 10 and seven ones to represent the 7. Finally, they were asked to combine the blocks to find out how much this was all together.

Nearly every teacher pushed the longs (tens) together first, and then combined the ones, so each had five longs and twelve ones. The majority then exchanged ten of the single units for another long (representing ten units), yielding six longs and two ones. Others just left the ones and counted them in that form (see Figures 5–2, 5–3, and 5–4).

After completing the hands-on activity, the teachers were handed paper and a pencil and were asked to make a step-by-step numerical record of what they did. They found this somewhat awkward since they were well versed in the traditional pencil-and-paper algorithm, but all agreed it was not truly difficult to combine the tens first, then the ones, even with pencil and paper. Doing so not only follows natural instincts, it also tends to cause the child (or adult) to focus on the value of the number using place value, rather than just reading the individual digits.

Given blocks, the child who has not fully developed her understanding of ten as a unit would approach the same problem in what she considers to be a perfectly normal way, combining the tens first, then the ones for another single ten. When the teacher tells her she

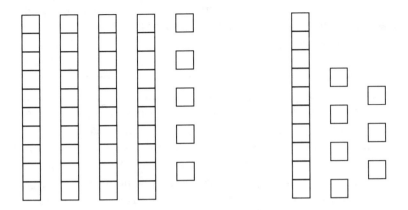

Figure 5–2 *45 is 4 longs and 5 ones. 17 is 1 long and 7 ones.*

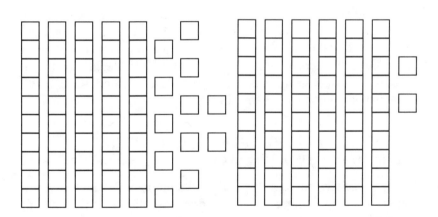

Figure 5–3 *Combine to 5 tens and 12 ones.*

Figure 5–4 *Exchange 10 of the ones for 1 long. 6 tens and 2 ones is 62.*

must follow a different procedure—add the ones first, then regroup, and finally add the tens—before she understands the process, what is she to do? She might rely on tricks she does not understand, but as in the case of Miko, this may not help her find a solution, especially not one that makes sense to her. Restricting instruction to traditional procedures does not honor the child's own thinking.

Lucky for Miko, she is in a class like Ms. Cohen-Hart's, where the teacher recognizes the subtleties in the mathematics content, and where children like Miko are provided enough time and hands-on experience to construct and share their own understanding of ideas.

Children should not be made to feel that their right ideas are wrong just because they are not traditional. Ms. Cohen-Hart worries, however, that her students will be burdened with inefficient, nontraditional methods. To test this, she and the others in her workshop group tried solving several additional problems using the left-to-right procedure, this time with three- and four-digit numbers. They were surprised to find that once they became comfortable with it, they were reasonably efficient. However, they also decided that once a child had the kind of understanding that inventing procedures generated, she would also be able to understand a more traditional procedure. They felt that they could find ways to move children to more efficient procedures, perhaps the traditional one. Over the years, Ms. Cohen-Hart has observed that when she asks the right questions and encourages children to try each others' ideas, most children decide for themselves that they prefer more efficient procedures, without being made to feel dependent on rote memorization.

UNDERSTANDING THE BACKGROUND, NEEDS, AND ABILITIES OF EACH STUDENT

Before a teacher can set up meaningful situations in which her students can build mathematics knowledge, she must first understand the individual backgrounds of her students.

Children enter school from a wide variety of situations. Many arrive at school fortified with an assortment of enriching experiences. They may have spent several years in a quality preschool setting, or at home with a caregiver who nurtured their language development and fostered their innate curiosity with books, trips, and a variety of experiences. Other children come from settings that are culturally different or that offer them few physical and social advantages. These children often arrive at school less prepared to meet the challenges of a conventional, English-speaking pre-K or kindergarten program. But while their observable and testable skills might make them appear less developed than others in the class, these children simply have had a different, and less traditional, set of experiences. In a child-centered classroom, nontraditional experiences can prove to be mathematically meaningful when seen and used appropriately. To do this, teachers must collect as much student information from as many sources as possible.

For children beyond kindergarten, school records and conversations with the previous year's teachers provide a variety of specific student data. Checking out the personal backgrounds of students helps teachers choose meaningful teaching strategies. It is important to know what is the primary language of the children and the children's families, and to be aware of any unusual home situations and the diversity of family structures. A school-based student profile may include standardized test scores, but anecdotal records and student portfolios present a broader picture of student behavior, physical and cognitive development, and academic achievement. Simply knowing the previous teacher's classroom strategies can help teachers determine how well children are prepared for the planned instructional program.

Although school records provide details and information, many teachers choose to assess the students for themselves in a variety of formal and informal ways. Children mature over the summer, gain specific knowledge without the help of organized instruction, and respond differently in different classroom settings. It does students a disservice to form expectations—especially negative ones—based on records or conversation alone. Engaging students in a variety of interesting activities during the first several weeks of the school year allows a teacher multiple opportunities to assess current language, math, reading, and writing skills, as well as to observe their general physical and social development.

In some schools, teachers conduct informal telephone conversations with parents early in the year to establish a line of communication with them as well as obtain background information that is valuable for planning classroom instruction. In addition, they often follow up with a letter to parents at home. The letter introduces the teacher and explains her mathematics program (see the kindergarten example in Figure 5–5).

In schools where many parents have difficulty reading or writing in English, teachers can replace the letter with a personal conversation,

Figure 5–5

Dear Parent/Guardian of _____:

As _____'s kindergarten teacher, I want to welcome you to our school family. I am looking forward to an exciting and rewarding year in which the students will learn many new things. In mathematics we will be studying beginning uses of numbers, shapes that are around us, what it means to measure things, patterns, addition and subtraction concepts, and many other exciting ideas.

I want to do everything I can to make sure that your child has a successful and pleasant year. You can help. Regularly talk to your child about school. Make your conversation friendly and informal. Ask questions that allow your child to openly describe the day's events. Encourage your child to be the "teacher" who teaches you what he/she learned in school.

If there is anything that you feel would be helpful for me to know as I work with your child, I would appreciate hearing from you. By working together, we can ensure your child has the best possible year.

If you have any questions now or at any time this year, please be sure to give me a call at 555-1111. I look forward to hearing from you.

Thank you for your help,

_____

(teacher's signature)

perhaps using volunteers who speak the language. Children from homes where English is not the primary language are often at a higher risk of failure in our school system. Knowing the backgrounds of these students allows teachers to include instructional approaches that encourage each student to talk about family and societal traditions.

Valuing the cultural diversity of the children allows the mathematics to contribute to a positive social atmosphere, and teachers in any school can incorporate a multicultural component into their curriculum. Instruction that appeals only to the customs of the majority culture puts many students at a disadvantage and deprives all students of enriching opportunities. Not only does a multicultural program broaden every child's cultural awareness and understanding, it provides even more opportunities to see mathematical ideas in different settings.

Those who teach in schools with diverse student backgrounds know firsthand that they must accommodate for the linguistic components of mathematics. Language structure and syntax are not universal and can cause confusion in understanding.

> Several of Allen Morton's second-grade students were counting coin values. Six children stood at the front of the room holding cards that showed three nickels and four pennies. Emilio, a child of Hispanic heritage, was asked how much money was shown.
>
> "Fifty-four cents," he responded.
>
> Mr. Morton called on another student who responded, "Nineteen cents." The second student was asked to show how he got his answer. He came forward and counted, "Five, ten, fifteen, sixteen, seventeen, eighteen, nineteen." Mr. Morton then asked Emilio for the amount again. "Fifty-four cents," he responded once more.
>
> The teacher asked Emilio to explain his method and he proceeded to count. "Five, ten, fifty, fifty-one, fifty-two, fifty-three, fifty-four." Mr. Morton could now see that Emilio was confused with the teen numbers. He knew that the English language practice of naming the ones value before the tens value only with the teen numbers is very difficult for many children, especially those from cultures where this is not the practice. The Spanish name for 15 is diez y cinco—10 and 5 with the 10 named first. Emilio's counting process was right on target; he simply needed help understanding the teen numbers. To him, fifteen sounded like five tens, or fifty.
>
> Mr. Morton asked the other children to work on a new problem. While they were doing that he asked Emilio to exchange each of the nickels for five pennies, and then count the amount as all pennies. Soon, Emilio was able to exchange the pennies for nickels again, and count out the nineteen cents.

How lucky for Emilio that his teacher took the time to have him explain his thinking, and that Mr. Morton understood both the math content and the cultural factors affecting Emilio's mathematics learning.

6

DEVELOPING A PLAN

It is the fortunate teacher, indeed, who finds herself in complete control of her classroom mathematics program. In reality, most public school teachers have the first step in planning handed to them in the form of a textbook or local curriculum. But although it may be true that local mandates dictate the general scope and sequence of the mathematics program, each teacher can, and must, look at the children, the setting, the textbook and/or curriculum, and place these within the context of her knowledge of what is developmentally appropriate for children and conducive to learning.

ONE TEACHER'S PLAN

Pamela Jackson teaches second grade in a large suburban school district. Teachers there are expected to follow the county's mathematics curriculum and are responsible for their students' mastery of many specific learning outcomes. Ms. Jackson enjoys teaching math and has always devoted at least an hour each day to mathematics instruction.

Believing she had no choice in the matter, Ms. Jackson's long-range plans used to come directly from the district's curriculum guide and her daily lessons came from the student texts and workbooks. This left her little room for creativity and little opportunity to individualize instruction in a way that met the needs of each student. Ms. Jackson's method was traditional: teach, review, test, then reteach if necessary. Like many teachers, she rarely made it through the book before the end of the year. Then she took part in a special program designed to help teachers understand and use the kinds of ideas found in the NCTM standards documents.

The program changed forever the way Ms. Jackson views, plans for, and incorporates mathematics into her teaching. She no longer relies solely on textbooks and workbooks. She now places her greatest emphasis on knowing her students and planning instruction that meets them where they are. She has added a greater variety of hands-on activities, problem-solving situations, and small- and large-group discussions into her program. There is still a specific "math time" every morning, but children now encounter math concepts throughout the day, from the morning's "early bird" activity to the time the children line up for the afternoon bus that will take them home. As a bonus, not only has Ms. Jackson been able to satisfy the main learning outcomes of her mandated curriculum, she is often able to take time at the end of the school year to explore new mathematics ideas.

Ms. Jackson is still responsible for teaching all content areas included in the district's second-grade mathematics curriculum, but the focus of her instruction has changed and so, consequently, has her method of planning. No longer does she flip open the curriculum guide to "Unit 1" to see what she will be teaching in early September, and no longer does she feel bound to follow the guide's sequence or timing. In fact, there are units she chooses to omit from her formal teaching plan altogether; she simply incorporates these concepts into her daily routines.

The first thing Ms. Jackson does when planning her math program for the year is to look at the curriculum guide and review what the "big ideas," or main concepts, are; then she determines which concepts will require the most time and how she can better develop these concepts through daily activities. In her first years of teaching Ms. Jackson would plan units and/or special lessons on graphs, patterns, numeration, odd and even numbers, and so on. Many concepts and skills, such as those central to graphing, and odd and even numbers, can be learned through daily activities. She continues to present numeration and patterns as separate units, but instructional time can be used more efficiently, and learning can be more solid, if daily activities regularly incorporate those concepts. Other content topics, such as measurement, time, and money, can also be introduced through incidental daily activities and then expanded on in specific units of instruction as needed. More difficult concepts—place value, multidigit computation, and fractions—require extensive, well-planned instructional units. In these areas, Ms. Jackson feels she must be certain her students have the numerous, progressive experiences that allow them to connect new concepts with prior knowledge and develop a strong foundation for building understanding.

Ms. Jackson begins the school year by familiarizing her students with the math routines and concepts they will encounter throughout second grade. They engage in a variety of informal graphing, patterning, and calendar activities; use manipulative materials; and speak the language of math. Ms. Jackson reserves the first month as a time to get to know her students and their current levels of progress. At the same time, her students spend the month gaining confidence as thinkers and doers of mathematics, for indeed, math is everywhere in Ms. Jackson's class.

A quick glance around the room on any given day affords just a hint of the numerous math activities the children will encounter. A large horizontal bar graph charts the children's favorite pizza. On the same wall hang directions on how to make patterns from names, a large calendar, a weather graph, a money chart, an "odd-even" box, and lots of student-drawn patterns. A number line along the top of the chalkboard counts toward the hundredth day of school. One easel displays a page of geometric shapes and equations and another holds a chart explaining how to graph the letters in the week's spelling words.

Ms. Jackson has developed an extensive repertoire of math activities to link her daily plans with the learning outcomes her students construct an understanding of in second grade. Each morning her students do an "early bird" activity when they enter the class. It may involve spinning a spinner and recording the data, or rolling a cube and recording the numbers that come before and after the number rolled. They also do a "graph of the day," creating and interpreting surveys of interest to them. Over the course of the year, they use bar graphs, line plots, pictographs, and Venn diagrams.

Three times a week they do the calendar. "Doing the calendar" in Ms. Jackson's class means more than just naming the day, date, and weather. It is a well-planned, multifaceted activity. Students place the date on the calendar, decide if it is odd or even, and talk about the patterns that emerge with each added number. They may do jumping jacks equal to the date, or handclaps equal to what they think the next day's date will be. "What will the date be on this day?" Ms. Jackson might ask, pointing to an empty square several days ahead. Or "What day will it be three days from now?" Children write answers on their individual slates and then discuss with a neighbor how they arrived at their answers. Then the children discuss it as a class.

"Early bird" activities in Ms. Jackson's classroom have children using a variety of materials independently.

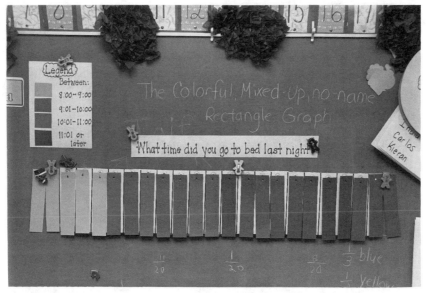

Ms. Jackson posts a new question each day for her students to graph.

Finally, they decide "how much the day is worth" by arranging various coin combinations to represent the monetary value of the day's date. One child might use a quarter to represent the twenty-fifth of the month while her neighbors use two dimes and a nickel, five nickels, or twenty-five pennies.

Planning ways to introduce these basic concepts in daily activities facilitates long-range planning. For example, in this class, students do a unit on money in January, but by the time January arrives, they have had numerous experiences with coins: they recognize the front and back of each coin, they know the names and values, and they have counted coin combinations. Because children can easily demonstrate the first objectives of the "money curriculum" before the unit even begins, they have ample time to work on the more complex learning outcomes, such as making change from a dollar.

Ms. Jackson has discovered that some content areas, such as graphing, do not require separate units at all. The children more than master the district's basic objectives—creating and interpreting simple bar graphs, picture graphs, and line plots—as a result of their daily graphing activities or through the mathematics that is integrated into their social studies or science units.

Name Sarah   Date _____
Think of all the different ways to make a triangle. ✗ Excellent

[Making Triangles with 20 Links]

Triangle 1	6 links (base)	7 links (side)	7 links (side)	side △ side =20 base	Work
Triangle 2	9 links (base)	5 links (side)	6 links side	side △ side =20 base	Great
Triangle 3	4 links (base)	8 links (side)	8 links (side)	side △ side =20 base	Great Thinking
Triangle 4	3 links (base)	9 links (side)	8 links (side)	side △ side =20 base	
Triangle 5	2 links (base)	8 links (side)	8 links (side)	side △ side = 20 base	
Triangle 6	5 links (base)	6 links (side)	9 links (side)	side △ side = 20 base	
Triangle 7	7 links (base)	6 links (side)	7 links (side)	△ = 20	

On the lines below write 2 things you noticed above.

I noticed that there is a lot of whys to make triangles with only 20 links. My hyest base number is 9. My hyest side number is 9 and my other hyest side number is 9 to.

Figure 6–1 *Ms. Jackson incorporates activities that combine geometry, addition, problem solving, and writing skills.*

When planning her units of math instruction, Ms. Jackson takes another look at the textbook and her county curriculum guide and evaluates the suggested lessons and how her students will relate to them. Many of the activities she finds are good ones, and she often adapts these to suit the needs of her multicultural class. She then maps out a number of other hands-on and problem-solving activities that will advance the children toward the intended math concept.

As is typical among second-grade classrooms, Ms. Jackson's group represents a wide range of ability and achievement, so she must plan activities to accommodate all students and strive to challenge each at his own level of understanding (see Figure 6–1).

Recently, she had her students writing equations from pattern blocks. The children traced blocks, counted the sides of each block, and then wrote equations that added the total numbers of sides. For example, a triangle (three sides) and a trapezoid (four sides) form the equation $3 + 4 = 7$. The class assignment was simply to choose five sets of pattern blocks and write five corresponding equations.

Even the least advanced students were able to complete the activity.

However, many were ready for more demanding work, and Ms. Jackson was able to adapt the lesson to accommodate them. One boy who was particularly ready for a challenge was asked to find and record as many combinations of blocks as he could that would total twenty-four sides. Doing this forced him to grapple with that number; he had to count by threes, fours, and even sixes, which are more difficult tasks than counting by twos or fives. He was even able to incorporate some early multiplication skills as he arranged various combinations of triangles, quadrilaterals, and hexagons to total twenty-four sides.

Ms. Jackson finds that planning has become second nature. She can easily determine which concepts her students grasp better in daily experiences and which require extensive time and detailed, focused activity. She doesn't feel rushed, and she no longer has trouble making it through the curriculum before the end of the school year. Best of all, she feels both she and her students are getting more out of the mathematics program by incorporating the principles of the NCTM standards.

ESTABLISHING A PLAN

Each classroom presents a unique blending of student backgrounds and personalities, teacher training and preference, and district curriculum mandates. It would be ideal if teachers fully knew the children before developing a plan for the school year. But as this is rarely the case, it is important that each teacher enters the year with a set of long-range goals and objectives that she would like to have students attain by the time they complete the grade. It is equally important that the teacher be prepared to adapt these goals into daily and weekly plans that reflect the needs of her particular students, enabling them to move successfully toward the desired outcomes.

Whether they have the autonomy to plan or are handed a specific curriculum to follow, teachers have many choices to make. Which concepts need to be taught and which are already known? Which are better taught in formal units and which informally in daily activities? Which concepts are most critical to these children? Which will be the most difficult and perhaps require the most time? What sequence will best allow the children to build on concepts they already have constructed for themselves? And what milestones should be set in order to reach the goals for the year?

The NCTM *Curriculum and Evaluation Standards* (1989) indicated that a primary-grade mathematics curriculum will "build beliefs about what mathematics is, about what it means to know and do mathematics, and about children's views of themselves as mathematics learners" (16). The *Principles and Standards* (2000) says much the same thing: "Young students are building beliefs about what mathematics is, about what it means to know and do mathematics, and about themselves as mathematics learners" (76). To accomplish these ends, it is necessary to modify the lessons in math texts or other prescribed curricula, to find connections with other subject areas, and to attempt to ground mathematics concepts in a variety of settings.

When setting a long-range plan it is helpful to review some basic assumptions for the curriculum as suggested by the *Curriculum and Evaluation Standards* (17–19), similar to, and supported by, ideas that the *Principles and Standards for School Mathematics* suggest. These assumptions can be used as guideposts for choosing content areas, determining specific teaching strategies, and deciding upon meaningful activities:

The mathematics curriculum should be conceptually oriented. Allowing children to build mathematical concepts requires time. When children succeed in memorizing rules or facts relatively quickly, but have little conceptual understanding of what these rules and facts represent, their teachers may believe the children can move quickly through the curriculum. But constructing *understanding* cannot be separated from meaningful experience. It is the development of meaningful experiences that must drive the instructional plan. The concepts that children build for themselves provide a foundation for new learning. A memorized rule or fact is quickly forgotten, but understanding has "staying power."

The mathematics curriculum should actively involve children in doing mathematics. If children are to build their mathematics understanding through meaningful experience, they must be doing real mathematics activities. This means solving problems that have meaning to them, using real materials, and having meaningful discourse with other children or adults. Children need planned activities that encourage them to explore, measure, weigh, compare, and construct a variety of objects, as well as ample opportunity to discuss ideas and predict solutions and reactions.

The mathematics curriculum should emphasize the development of children's mathematical thinking and reasoning

abilities. The standards documents emphasize the need for children to develop confidence in their ability to think mathematically and to communicate their thinking. Confident children will be better prepared to solve problems and analyze data. To develop this confidence, the *Principles and Standards* urges, "Therefore, it is imperative to provide all students with high-quality programs that include significant mathematics presented in a manner that respects both the mathematics and the nature of young children" (p. 76).

The mathematics curriculum should emphasize the application of mathematics. The ultimate purpose of learning mathematical content is not to complete the exercises at the end of a textbook chapter or to pass a minimal grade competency test before June. Rather, mathematics procedures are real-world processes that help children solve problems in their everyday lives. Classroom activities that build on data collection and interpretation prepare children to meet these demands.

The mathematics curriculum should include a broad range of content. Careful planning is necessary to include the full spectrum of mathematical processes, especially when it is not directly laid out in mandated texts or curricula. Young children benefit from experiences with measurement, geometry, statistics, probability, and algebra. Textbooks and curriculum guides often pay little or no attention to these branches of mathematics, and teachers who are new to presenting these concepts may lack confidence in their ability to include them (or their students' capacity to comprehend them) in the primary grades. But informal introduction is not difficult.

A program based on the mathematics standards will be student driven and should include a set of long-range plans that address content goals and student needs. The traditional way to use textbooks—to begin with Chapter 1 and continue through to whatever chapter the class happens to reach at the end of the school year—does not facilitate a student-centered curriculum. This does not mean that a text is not useful. Many books, especially newer ones, have interesting activities that can be adapted to suit students' needs.

To begin the school year, teachers can develop or select instructional units that are motivating and relatively free of prerequisites. This allows the first few weeks to serve as a reentry and warm-up for students after the summer break. This also serves as an assessment period, during which the teacher can determine students' strengths and weaknesses and establish productive routines for math. By watching students in familiar situations, asking probing questions that bring out their thinking, observing their work, and reflecting on their understanding, the teacher, with or without a text, is better able to map out more detailed plans related to her goals for the year, the needs of the children, and local mandates.

Ms. Jackson involved her students in many patterning and graphing activities in the beginning of the year. Geometry and measurement activities are excellent starting points. Informal geometry is enjoyable to children and provides opportunities for patterning, comparing, analyzing, and deriving numbers from shapes.

One of Ms. Jackson's colleagues uses a highly motivational geometry activity that accomplishes two objectives. It has children investigating quantity, shape, and how objects correspond with one another, and at the same time, it establishes a routine for children to work together cooperatively. To initiate the activity, pairs of children choose seven pattern blocks of at least three different shapes. They arrange the blocks in any design or interesting shape with no interior holes. Some students create interesting symmetric and asymmetric designs; others make recognizable shapes—a vehicle, animal, or monster. One member of the pair holds the design while the other traces around the outside. The student pairs exchange outlines and work to discover which blocks were used to create other students' designs. It isn't long before children discover that there can be more than one way to make the same design and are encouraged to discuss their findings with the original artists.

In the next step, the children try to fill in the outline with more or fewer than seven blocks. Soon numbers of edges, sizes of angles, and comparisons of shapes begin to enter into students' conversation. Finally, students devise ways to record the shapes used, the numbers of blocks, and the numbers of edges, and to compare their records with those of their classmates.

Measurement activities are a ready source of numbers for basic computation—numbers to add, subtract, compare, or use to make fractions. As Ms. Valentine observed the day her students weighed and compared their chicks (Chapter 3), when children make their own measurements and then use these measurements for problem-solving tasks, numbers and computation take on real meaning. The activity and the numbers it uses are inherently motivating. Especially

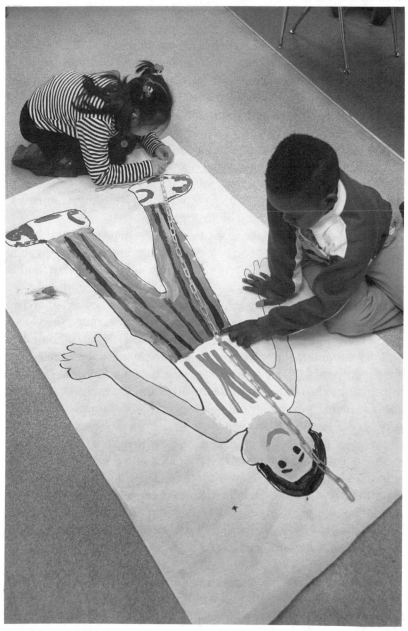

Measurement activities can be incorporated into many areas of the primary math curriculum and are a great way to integrate science, social studies, and art. They can be useful as "get acquainted" activities at the beginning of the year, and can serve as a means of assessment.

DEVELOPING A PLAN

at the beginning of the year, measurement can be a natural extension of many "get acquainted" activities, and can be incorporated into the curriculum while familiarizing students with their new classroom environment.

Geometry, measurement, and other familiar, yet motivating, activities provide a set of lenses through which the teacher can observe the students. The teacher can ask many questions and collect and record student data. How do these children work together? What vocabulary do they incorporate into their "math talk," and is it utilized appropriately? Are they confident in their ability to accomplish mathematical tasks? To what extent can they collect, interpret, and display data? Can they use simple problem-solving strategies? Do they have the background for the mathematical concepts we plan to cover?

Insights that are gained into the students' thinking about the mathematics can then be used to make decisions about the sequence and emphases for the various topics that will be addressed during the year. Starting the year with a textbook, which usually opens with one or two chapters of review, does not adequately supply these important pieces of student information. In fact, opening the year with review is usually a waste of valuable instructional time. Children do forget things over the summer, but opening with interesting topics will help bring some of that back into memory, and any additional needed review can be accomplished much more efficiently at the time it is needed for new learning. More important, beginning the year with review does not provide the motivation needed to help students move into new ideas with enthusiasm and confidence.

Once she is familiar with the skills and needs of the class, the teacher is ready to devise or adjust a long-range scheme for the year and to project time frames for the various units that address the main mathematical ideas. A long-range plan that is conceptually oriented addresses broad concepts for the students to experience over the course of the school year. Once again, the NCTM standards documents can assist the teacher who is new to developing this type of mathematics program. The process standards of the *Principles and Standards*—Problem Solving, Reasoning and Proof, Communication, Connections, and Representation—provide a direction for the instructional strategies to be used. The content standards indicate content-specific areas of mathematics that need to be addressed in the instructional program in grades pre-K–2 and 3–5: Number and Operations, Algebra, Geometry, Measurement, and Data Analysis.

Connecting these concept areas with the text or local curriculum guidelines can help to establish a general plan for the year. A sample kindergarten plan might begin something like this:

September
geometry; games with counting; sorting, collecting, and displaying data; *above, below*

October
counting activities; making sets; identifying sets by number; *more, less, same;* ordering sets

November
exploring lengths with nonstandard units; comparing data

December
using numerals; investigating time and money; concept of addition

Ongoing
language development; attendance activities; calendar activities; number sense; problem-solving skills and applications; ongoing use of previously learned concepts

Each successive grade should build on concepts that were initiated in the previous year. A sample plan for a second-grade program might begin like this:

September
collecting and interpreting data; reading the story of a graph; relating numbers on a number line to numbers in a hundreds chart; solving addition story problems

October
inventing procedures for solving addition and subtraction story problems; symmetry and reflection in geometry; place value

November
numeration and place value concepts; two-digit addition and subtraction; time

December
measurement; interpreting and constructing graphs; story problems to introduce the concept of multiplication

Ongoing
calendar and attendance number concepts; basic fact strategies for addition and subtraction; number sense; graphing; problem solving

Every teacher must develop her own plan tailored to meet the demands of the district curriculum and/or text and adjusted for the needs of her students. The samples provided are simply examples of what a plan might look like.

Short-Range Planning
Once the teacher has established a general conceptual framework, she can put the content into unit plans and then select specific instructional strategies that address these major ideas.

The first step to planning a unit is to look at the math content. Specific content, often defined in the curriculum guide or textbook in terms of instructional objectives or learning outcomes, needs to be placed in the context of the students' individual needs and the specific collective needs of the class. What did students study in previous units or previous years? At what point are they functioning now? Are there linguistic or social factors that will influence learning?

The teacher can then design a plan of instructional activities that focuses on concept development. This general plan need not be elaborate. It primarily serves as a guidepost that can be adjusted frequently to accommodate student progress. The teacher can often find appropriate activities in the curriculum guide, student textbook, teacher manual, or other available resources. Lessons can be adapted to fit the needs of each class population.

Teachers who primarily use textbooks as entry points for their scope and sequence plans can still creatively adapt text activities to their individual classroom needs. Consider, for example, a textbook that describes an outdoor activity in which children make a variety of triangles and quadrilaterals and then record their characteristics. Children, representing vertices (corners), hold a rope, linking themselves together. They record in pictures the many kinds of triangles and quadrilaterals they can make with a given length of rope.

Even though the curriculum guide and text recommend beginning the year with recognition of numerals, a teacher in northern Minnesota might need to use this geometry activity in September, before the weather gets too cold for children to be outdoors. She might choose to do the activity in the fall and use the recorded pictures for a classroom introduction to the meaning and symbolic representation of 3 and 4. The recorded shapes can be duplicated with three and four rods of various lengths in the classroom. After other numerals have been introduced, the children can continue the outdoor activity by making models of polygons with five, six, seven, or more sides and vertices. The teacher can use the recorded results to help young children investigate order (*more than, less than, the same as*), addition and subtraction facts, and even measurement and identification of various polygons in the world about them. To add challenge to the activity, the teacher might encourage the children to use combinations of two or more pattern blocks to make a variety of shapes with four, five, six, or more sides. Or they could use the rope to investigate shapes with no corners. How would they hold the rope to make these shapes? How many such shapes can there be? Could they create a shape with one or two corners?

In interpreting unit plans into daily activities, careful attention must be given to how well a selected activity brings out the mathematics. In classrooms incorporating the NCTM standards, teachers usually provide several hands-on experiences with concrete materials before pencil-and-paper activity, and allow ample opportunity for students to discuss individual problem-solving strategies with other children and interested adults.

Although it's true that children have the greatest opportunity to build accurate and useful mathematics concepts when the activities are engaging and developmentally appropriate, many "fun" activities have little mathematical potential. In other activities, the mathematical potential may not be realized unless the teacher carefully thinks it through in advance, and uses good questions to promote thoughtful discussion.

For instance, students can use base-ten blocks to perform addition or subtraction. However, if they see the purpose of this as getting the answer, then they will not gain what they should from the activity. The blocks should never become an alternative way to get answers, but should be used as a way to help children think about numbers. Children should record their block work on paper, using numbers and operation symbols. Those children able to do computation without the use of manipulatives should only be asked to use blocks when modeling their thinking for the teacher. If the connection between the modeling with the blocks and the written procedure is not made, then the blocks become a second algorithm to be learned, a burden, rather than a support for developing understanding and learning a paper-and-pencil procedure.

Many teachers find it beneficial to begin each unit with a day of activities that review concepts essential to understanding the unit. This can serve two purposes: students can remember and sharpen previously acquired content knowledge by revisiting old concepts, and the teacher can assess the students' present functional level. Test results and anecdotal records that show student achievement at the end of a previous instructional unit may no longer hold true, since children often grow in conceptual understanding without the aid of direct instruction.

As Ms. Jackson discovered, planning daily lessons should not be done too far in advance because plans need to be regularly revised. Armed with information gained through observations of students during daily activities, she fine-tunes her plans as often as necessary. Should this activity be extended? For whom was it too difficult? Who needs additional support? Are the students bored and ready to move on to more challenging problems?

Sticking to the Plan

Each teacher needs to experiment with different methods of mathematics planning in order to find the best course of action for her teaching approach and classroom situations. Teachers new to the methods set forth in the standards of the NCTM may find that failure to establish a strong long-range plan can increase the risk they will drop their newfound approach.

Traditional direct instruction often brings tangible, testable (albeit sometimes fleeting) results early in the school year, and teachers used to more didactic teaching methods initially may be alarmed by a lack of concrete evidence of student achievement. Midway through the first year of her new program, Ms. Jackson began to worry. She remembered student test-and-drill performances of previous years. This year's students appeared less proficient in pencil-and-paper computation. It was clear she was not moving through the curriculum as rapidly as before, and she worried that her class would not make it through the year's math program.

But then she remembered that in other years she had given her students facts to memorize, clearly defined algorithms to use, and specific skills to perform. They retained too little, and were not able to discuss what they were doing. Now, while providing them with a strong mathematics foundation, progress was taking a little more time and was a little more difficult to ascertain.

As her January money unit rolled around, she noticed how smoothly it went. Students were better prepared to tackle the most difficult aspects of the unit than students in previous years. Other math content areas seemed to benefit equally. She noticed that students used the vocabulary of math throughout the day and that they appeared self-assured and confident in their abilities to solve problems.

A different kind of progress was taking hold. After careful observation and student-teacher discussions, Ms. Jackson realized that her students had a deeper conceptual understanding and were better able to transfer that understanding to new situations. It was apparent that making the students more responsible for explaining their thinking and justifying their answers was paying dividends.

Before long, students were producing positive, testable results, and she was surprised to discover that her class covered all the mandated content objectives with time to spare. Given the opportunity to build concepts, habits, and confidence early, her students were able to move quickly through the more difficult units they encountered later in the year. This was an added bonus for her—one that she cashed in on by letting her students explore unscheduled content areas, solve logic problems, and reinforce their learning through motivating math games.

Giving students the opportunity to develop concepts and their own methods of solving problems requires patience, flexibility, and time. The payoff is stronger mathematical concept development and increased retention. Once students have established basic math concepts, they will move through the curriculum more quickly, with greater confidence, with a higher rate of success, and with the ability to transfer these concepts to new content.

A general rule that might guide daily instruction is: "If it doesn't make sense to the children, why are they doing it?" Instructional plans should always relate to big ideas of mathematics. Some programs break the mathematical concepts into small, discrete steps to be taught separately, like adding ingredients into a recipe. With a recipe, the result may be delicious bread, but with mathematics the result is often a series of narrowly defined steps that do not necessarily support or develop conceptual understanding. Programs that focus on the main idea and use problem solving as the basis for moving toward that goal will meet the needs of far more students than piecemeal programs. They provide greater likelihood that all students will learn the mathematics, not just a few.

Spontaneity vs. Planning

A student-centered curriculum that gives learners the opportunity to develop their own methods of solving problems in meaningful situations necessitates flexible planning. Often the greatest motivation to learn occurs as a result of spontaneous events that happen in and around the classroom. At the same time, mathematics instruction cannot be totally extemporaneous and unplanned.

Occasionally, teachers modify their daily plans to take advantage of unexpected events, but they might want to think about why they developed a plan in the first place. Long-range planning is essential to implementing a program that encourages students to think mathe-

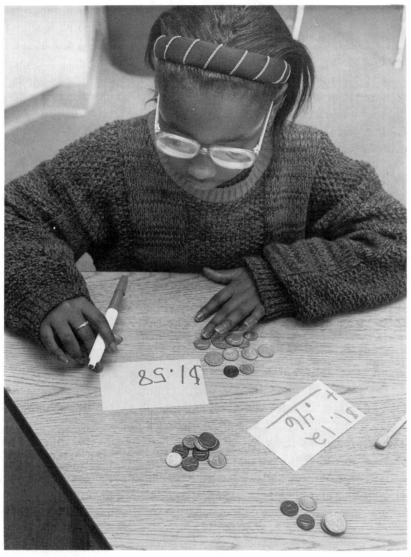

Like those in Ms. Jackson's class, students who are given the opportunity to build a strong mathematics foundation are able to tackle difficult problems with confidence.

matically. Educators agree that mathematics has a specific body of content that should be developed in a planned sequence, and teachers who use a long-range plan for the year can safely assume that an adequate range of important ideas is being explored.

When planning relies too heavily on serendipity and too little on adherence to a logical mathematical sequence, mathematics learning can get off track. It becomes easy to miss or gloss over content in an attempt to seize the opportunity of the moment. However, if the long-range plan is firmly established, and the desired learning outcomes continue to guide activities, it becomes easy to adapt daily lessons to fit timely topics. Place value, fractions, or statistics can be taught in the context of current events—the Olympic games, a new class pet, or even a new event that has affected families in the community.

Planning for Math in an Integrated Curriculum

Placing mathematics instruction within the context of other curricular areas helps make sense of math concepts, establishes a value for math content, and gives meaning to the other disciplines. Thematic planning—planning interdisciplinary units around broad or specific themes (transportation, raising baby chicks, setting up a recycling project) can incorporate math, science, reading, language arts, and social studies, as well as art, music, and physical education. Math can serve as a tool to make sense of the other areas. Students use measurement, graphing, and statistics to collect, record, and interpret social and scientific data. The use of fractions, estimation, and number operations is inherent in scientific procedures.

The scope and sequence of the math content must be evident in the overall plan of an integrated curriculum. Often it is the science or social studies that drives an interdisciplinary unit and math becomes a peripheral issue. If, for example, a teacher chooses a weather topic as the theme for a unit, he may concentrate on the science content and use reading, writing, and math as tools to accomplish specific science objectives. Math may be used every day during this unit, but unless the specific mathematics concepts defined in the long-range plan are addressed, the students may fail to progress mathematically.

But frequently, the sequence of the science content is less critical than the sequence of the mathematics content. Specific objectives in a weather unit, for example, can be studied at any point in the year. To most effectively develop the potential of the mathematics involved in this unit, formal weather study might be shifted to the latter half of the year, when students have had many experiences with fractions, graphing, and measurement and are ready for a unit on interrelating units of measurement. Of course, as with many areas of mathematics, some of the weather objectives might best be spread over the school year, and tied into other curricular areas accordingly. By looking carefully at the skills needed in a science or social studies unit, and then matching them with the skills the students have acquired and/or are currently working on, teachers can develop interdisciplinary units that enhance both the mathematics curriculum and the other content areas.

7
....

IMPLEMENTING THE PROGRAM

Rosa, Tyrone, and the other children described in this text attend schools that are implementing the NCTM standards in their math curriculum. These schools are located in a fairly typical urban area, where teachers and children must cope daily with the socioeconomic effects associated with low-income districts. But despite the environment around these schools, students are achieving in math. Teachers are rethinking their strategies, restocking their shelves and cupboards, and retooling their classrooms to address the goals set by the standards. Most of all, they are proving that these methods can be implemented in any school or classroom.

If the best elements from each of these schools were combined, they would form a model school-community committed to excellence in mathematics—a school in which children are encouraged to value and use math in personal terms. What might a visitor walking down the hall of a model school find? Brightly decorated walls sporting student art and colorful posters, many displaying mathematical concepts. Outside one first-grade class, the hum of children's voices is punctuated by an occasional exclamation or laugh. The teacher's voice can be heard in gentle conversation with several children, rising in inquiry and then pausing as the smaller voices respond.

A peek inside reveals walls covered with charts, graphs, posters, and calendars. Magnetic name tags are distributed across three sectors on an attendance Venn diagram. Clear containers holding various blocks, links, and cubes are stacked on shelves beside books, microscopes, geoboards, and several sets of scales. The children, huddled in small groups, bend intently over their work.

A closer examination reveals the source of their activity. Each group shares a colorfully sewn cloth sack, bulging with blocks. One partner shakes the bag and the second reaches in and pulls out a block. Another child records its color on a graph and returns the block to the bag. The teacher visits each group and asks questions that help the students see relationships among collected data. "What color block did you get the most of?" "Why do you think that happened?" "Which color did you get the least of?" "Do you think there are more red, blue, or yellow blocks in the bag?" "Why?" "If you did this again, which color do you think you'd pull out most often?" "Now fill a bag and predict what color blocks you would choose most often."

Continuing on through the school wing, a visitor might note the variety of lessons and learning strategies evident in the classrooms. In one room, children are busy writing and exchanging their own addition story problems, while the class next door works on place value. These children are working with base-ten blocks using numbers that came from a physical education activity. In another classroom, children are voting on the book they'll be reading later that day and using Post-it notes to add their names to a wall chart. In still another class, busy hands deftly measure desks, books, and cubbies and then record the data in notebooks.

Naturally, each activity has been set up differently. Student background experiences, performance levels, and personalities vary. Teachers put their own signatures on their programs in ways that highlight individual preferences and strengths. But despite the obvious differences, there are key elements common to all classrooms successfully implementing the NCTM standards. In these classrooms, teachers informally assess student progress throughout the day. They take care to value each child's learning style and individual approach to math problems, no matter how far from the traditional path it may wind. In addition, these mathematics programs have children

- solving problems in meaningful situations
- using manipulatives
- working cooperatively with others in small groups
- developing their own procedures, which they can discuss, explain, modify, write about, and value
- explaining their thinking
- listening to each other share strategies
- using thinking strategies to learn basic facts
- encountering math throughout their curriculum—in language and reading, social studies and science, and even art and physical education

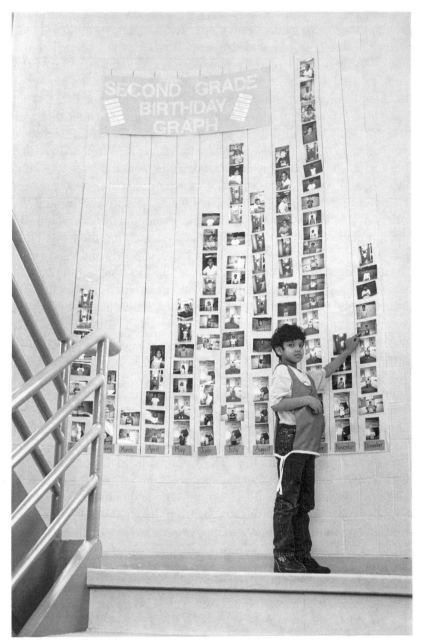

Evidence of mathematics can be found everywhere in schools implementing the NCTM standards.

IMPLEMENTING THE PROGRAM

SOLVING PROBLEMS IN MEANINGFUL SITUATIONS

Solving problems must be the focus of any mathematics instructional program. Teachers will see in the *Principles and Standards* that five process standards have been provided to guide instruction. Problem solving is the first of the process standards:

> Instructional programs from prekindergarten through grade 12 should enable all students to:
> * build new mathematical knowledge through problem solving
> * solve problems that arise in mathematics and in other contexts
> * apply and adapt a variety of appropriate strategies to solve problems
> * monitor and reflect on the process of mathematical problem solving (116)

The other process standards are closely related to, and support, problem solving:

> reasoning and proof
> communication
> connections
> representation

Reasoning and Proof

Young children use reasoning naturally and intuitively, but it is essential that this ability be recognized by teachers and supported by the mathematics curriculum. There is some evidence (Carpenter and Moser 1983) that children's use of intuitive reasoning diminishes as they progress through the early grades. This decrease may, to some extent, be attributable to instructional practices that require children to solve problems by prescribed routines or algorithms, rather than encouraging them to think through problems, using their knowledge and experience to invent their own procedures. When children look to rules, they are not exercising their natural abilities to reason and solve problems. When good reasoning skills are developed, students can attain the level at which they can say they have "proven" their idea to be true using the mathematics that they previously understood. Good reasoning leads to proof.

Communication

Communication, especially oral communication, contributes to the learning process. Like Danielle (Chapter 3), who benefited from "talking through" a problem, children who think through what they have done—carefully enough to describe it clearly to others—strengthen their own mathematical understanding.

Connections

Conceptual understanding is developed as learners make connections among related ideas. Mathematics concepts need to be linked to other math concepts and to key elements central to other disciplines. Science, social studies, art, and physical education form a concrete framework on which children can hook abstract mathematics processes and concepts. Conversely, mathematics provides a language for communicating about and explaining phenomena that occur across disciplines and throughout the school day.

Representation

Originally, NCTM included representation as part of communication, but the revised document recognizes that representation is much more than communication. It is interrelated with, but separate from, all other process standards. Children reinforce and demonstrate their understanding when they translate mathematical concepts and procedures into representations, drawings, and physical models, or are able to construct word problems that fit specific concepts. Student-generated 2-D, 3-D, and textual models provide them with physical materials and mental images for exploring mathematics concepts. The mere act of representation enhances learning.

Because problem solving is so important to setting the stage, developing, and then applying mathematical understanding, it's important for teachers to consistently interrelate it with the other four process standards. Children need to be placed in problem-solving situations that lead them to develop their own ideas and understandings. In the early grades, these can come directly from the students' daily routines and experiences. Such child-centered situations appeal to the inherent egocentricity of youngsters, and they encourage students to see the value of mathematics in their everyday lives.

It is the teacher's role to select or create activities that will be meaningful for her students and then flush out the mathematical potential from these activities. Real-world activities such as cooking; building something for the classroom; or selecting, dividing, and distributing materials for a class party are examples that are inherently interesting to children and hold tremendous instructional possibilities (see Figure 7–1).

The problem was we had
to get 100 dinosaur out
of a cup. Then everybody
had a turn to try to even
all the dinosaurs up so
everybody would have an
even number. Then Ms. Fox
came over and took kevin's
place. Then I got another idea
to put all the dinosaurs in

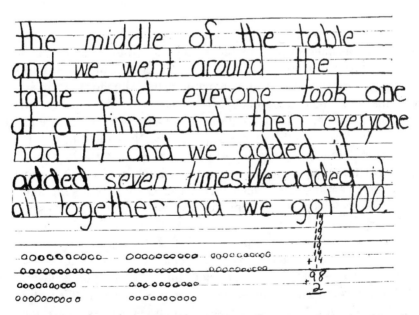

the middle of the table
and we went around the
table and everyone took one
at a time and then everyone
had 14 and we added it
added seven times. We added it
all together and we got 100.

Figure 7–1 *When children are placed in creative problem-solving situations, they
are driven to develop their own procedures, ideas, and understandings.*

Being receptive to student-generated questions can lead teachers to the most meaningful activities of all. As children investigate their own questions at their own pace, they are primed for discovery; they seek meaning in their own worlds. Time spent thoroughly investigating a few high-interest problems can prove to be more productive than completing many low-interest problems that do not incorporate adequate discussion about discoveries, processes, and results.

"Meaningful problems" do not always need to be real-world problems, but instead could be those that use manipulative materials, such as Popsicle sticks, pattern blocks, or tangrams; story problems that appeal to a child's imagination; or activities that connect math with other disciplines. Even ordinary computation can be treated as a problem to be solved when the question is focused on the ways to solve, rather than on just getting the right answer. Any problem with no prescribed solution method that invites exploration by students can yield good thinking and learning. When the students in one class graphed the vowels and consonants in their spelling lists, they became curious whether there was a pattern from one week's list to the next. The ensuing investigation was taken on by a small group of children who shared their findings with the rest of the class, updating their data weekly.

Story problems are often used to motivate the development of specific mathematical concepts. They encourage children to use their intuitive reasoning to build an understanding of the mathematics that is usually much deeper than that achieved by teaching procedures directly. For example, one difficult mathematical situation for primary- and many intermediate-level children occurs when the starting number is not known. Students might be given a problem like "Alice had some toy dinosaurs. She gave 8 to Jeremy. Now Alice has 15 toy dinosaurs. How many toy dinosaurs did Alice have to start with?" Because the action in the story is one of giving something away, most children will immediately think this is a subtraction problem, rather than one of addition. Helping children find ways to put themselves into the story, perhaps by drawing or manipulating real objects, not only leads to a solution for the problem, it also encourages the development of good problem-solving strategies that can be applied to many problems and a more complete understanding of real-world mathematics-related situations. Some teachers have done this by first having the students look at the story as an art activity where they make a drawing to show what is happening, with the various number combinations then being related to the drawing.

No matter how motivating or interesting the setting, one should not assume that children will automatically get mathematical meaning from every classroom activity. Frequent teacher-student, student-student, and whole-group discussions assist both conceptual understanding and language development, often with the teacher guiding the direction of the discussions through thoughtful comments and probing questions. Students become independent thinkers and problem solvers when they are prodded with open-ended questions: "What strategies do you think might work to find a solution?" "What were you thinking when you solved that problem?" "Is your answer reasonable, and how can you decide if it is?"

USING MANIPULATIVES

Learning theory suggests that children's mathematics knowledge often begins with actions involving objects. Conceptual understanding begins with the concrete (using objects to model), moves to the semi-concrete (pictorial or representational), and then moves to the abstract (mental or symbolic).

Many children learn to identify numerals, or can rote count to relatively high numbers at an early age. "Five," exclaims one young child when shown that numeral. "Hear me count," commands another who proceeds in rapid fire, "one, two, three, four, five." Despite these early performances, many teachers (and even many parents) realize that young children often have little "number sense," that they don't fully understand numbers and number processes. Before children can *understand* 5, they must first discover "fiveness." They must encounter multiple sets of five—five blocks, five crayons, five shoes, five children. They must handle five, they must count five, they must be able to divide it up and then put it back together again. They must associate in one-to-one correspondence five cookies, five plates, and five children. In essence, they cannot understand the abstract meaning of five, or even associate what the numeral 5 represents, until they have had multiple experiences with concrete objects and many opportunities to relate five to other numbers.

Manipulatives provide the props with which children explore mathematics concepts. With concrete materials in hand, they can experiment, build, add, divide, weigh, measure, and compare. They can develop and apply abstract ideas, make hypotheses, and test ideas. They have props that invite reflection, stimulate and facilitate conversation, and assist explanation.

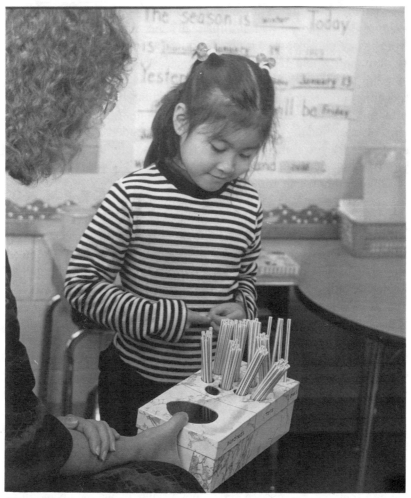

Manipulative materials provide the props with which children can experiment, build, add, divide, weigh, measure, and compare.

A variety of materials should be available for children as they move through their mathematics program. The NCTM standards suggest that primary-grade classrooms be equipped with counters: interlocking cubes; connecting links; base-ten, attribute, and pattern blocks; tiles; geometric models; rulers; spinners; colored rods; geoboards; balances; fraction pieces; and graph, grid, and dot paper. While more expensive materials are often kept in a central location so that classrooms can share their use, a variety of items should be kept in each classroom so children can benefit from daily use. For example, connecting cubes in prekindergarten, kindergarten, and first grade, or place value materials in second through fifth grades, should be available for easy access.

For the many schools that do not have the funds to equip each room with a variety of supplies, homemade materials can prove to be as good as or better than those produced commercially. For example, dried lima beans spray-painted on one side make excellent two-color counters. Having children or their families contribute or even construct materials is a fun and easy way to get parents, grandparents, and siblings involved. Constructing materials, which often involves measurement and computation skills, offers the added benefit of providing valuable learning experiences for children at home or in school. Many mathematics educators believe that drawing can be substituted for some manipulatives and the results will be as good as or better than using physical materials. This may, for example, be true for learning fraction concepts, since the student who draws to solve a problem may get a better sense of what the whole is (e.g., Empson 1995).

Manipulating images and symbols through computer software also seems to help children learn concepts that are typically introduced through hands-on materials (e.g., Clements and Sarama 2000). Some mathematical ideas that are difficult to show with physical manipulatives, such as any problem that involves action related to subtraction, can be shown on the computer. Manipulating materials to model subtraction can be a complex action for young children. Blocks do not move themselves. They must be moved *by* someone. For example, a child might have trouble using manipulatives to solve the following problem: "Destiny had 23 candies. Then she gave some to Deanna. Now Destiny has 15 candies. How many candies did Destiny give to Deanna?" Since the amount given away and the 15 that are left are both a part of the 23 that Destiny had to start with, it is difficult to show this problem clearly with physical materials. The computer, on the other hand, can show those events by depicting the action. Few teachers would want to rely totally on computers for instruction, but when the hardware and software are available, the computer offers a viable alternative.

Students who have little or no experience using manipulatives will probably require some special support before they use the materials effectively. Many children, for example, misunderstand base-ten blocks. Some of these students see ten ones glued together as just another "single" block of a different size. These children are simply not ready to use the blocks. Others have not had enough experience with blocks that can be taken apart and put together to understand the place value arrangement from ones to tens to hundreds. They will need more help from teachers and other students to interpret the blocks before they can use them effectively.

Using manipulatives often requires, and can be used to help develop, student responsibility. Some materials, such as the rubber bands used with geoboards, seem to lend themselves to misuse. Many teachers have found that pairing students who are more easily distracted with those who are more responsible may ward off problems before they begin; enforcing a strict "misuse leads to no use" policy usually alleviates problems (with time). An alternative to denying manipulatives to all students, or even some students, is to have those who misuse blocks use substitutes made out of colored construction paper. The children will be able to participate in the same explorations as the children using the real blocks. As students become more familiar with the daily use of geoboards, blocks, and links, the novelty of handling materials diminishes and more time and energy can be devoted to their application in a creative and interesting mathematics learning environment.

The teachers in Chris Valentine's school discovered several management techniques that helped foster responsible use of materials. As children were given opportunities to share strategies and invent procedures, they began to feel that they had some control over the mathematics. That, in itself, seemed to lead to more responsible use of the materials. When children were using materials to solve real-world problems that they understood and wanted to solve, materials use improved. Finally, the teachers often offered students choices. For example, they might direct the children, "You can use manipulatives, paper and pencil, or do it in your mind." Providing students with a sense of autonomy—control over their own learning—produced greater personal responsibility.

Introducing manipulatives one at a time gives children a chance to become familiar with the characteristics and uses of each new set of materials. Students need time to explore the manipulatives on their own before being asked to use the materials in activities designated by the teacher. Some teachers ask students to think of as many uses as they can for new materials. This enhances student exploration and allows children a chance to gain confidence without experiencing stress or failure. Additionally, observing students while they explore

IMPLEMENTING THE PROGRAM

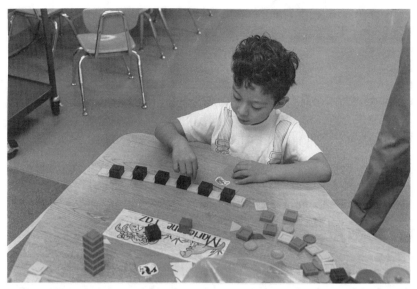

The availability of a variety of math materials helps ensure opportunities for children to develop their own procedures with understanding.

can provide the teacher with insight into the children's mathematical maturity and individual creativity. (This is also an appropriate time for teachers to establish ground rules or for students to get some of the less mathematical "experimenting" out of the way.)

Having students take turns distributing, checking, and collecting materials on a daily basis helps build responsibility. Wall charts and daily assignment cards can be used to assign and keep track of whose job it is to pass out or clean up materials. Proper storage helps ease the distribution and collection of materials. Lunch trays or sample carpet squares prevent pieces from falling off desks and can reduce the noise associated with students working with blocks on a hard surface.

Assigning children to pairs or small groups often facilitates classroom management. It allows the teacher to work with fewer children at a time, helps her monitor the use of materials, and makes it easier to monitor student understanding. In classrooms that are not well equipped, this method also reduces the quantity of materials needed for the group.

It must be noted that providing manipulative materials is not educational in and of itself. Children must be placed in meaningful situations—those that pose interesting problems and provide opportunities for personal reflection and peer interaction—for concrete materials to foster growth in mathematics concepts. If the mathematics isn't drawn out of the manipulative activity, then the manipulative material may become an alternative way of solving, rather than a tool for learning mathematics. Good questioning and recording strategies must be used to bring out the mathematics. Helping children learn to record their thinking with numbers and symbols through questioning and modeling is an important aspect of manipulative use.

WORKING COOPERATIVELY

Math is not a spectator sport. In order to learn mathematics, children need to be active participants in doing and discussing mathematics. Working in pairs and/or small groups, then, is almost essential to effective student learning. Because children are naturally social, group processes can easily play a fundamental part in primary-grade mathematics programs. They enable each child to speak, listen, and work cooperatively with others in the learning process.

Traditional classrooms have one speaker (often the teacher or a highly verbal child) and twenty-five or so listeners. In these scenarios, only one child is an active participant, while all others are relegated to the passive role of listeners (if they are even doing that). Child-centered classrooms often function under a different model, incorporating cooperative grouping activities throughout the day. When a class of twenty-five students is divided into groups of two or four, there can be up to twelve speakers actively involved at any one time, and twelve listeners poised and ready to respond.

Cooperative learning strategies provide opportunities to grow socially, analytically, and conceptually. Solving problems with others demands that students inquire, explore, analyze, explain, challenge, justify, modify, interpret, and communicate their ideas effectively, working together to solve a common problem.

Group activities can lead to a better development of mathematical understanding because of the communication that must occur for the group to function. Ideally, these activities necessitate that children use all four components of language skills: speaking, listening, reading, and writing. As children communicate in a mathematical problem-solving activity, they must incorporate the language of math. They break down intuitive thoughts into step-by-step plans and processes, concretizing concepts for themselves as they explain them to others.

IMPLEMENTING THE PROGRAM

Planning action, making diagrams, describing shapes, comparing sizes, predicting outcomes, and explaining solutions require students to make the kind of connections between abstract concepts and verbal or graphic symbols that build a strong mathematical foundation.

Children's independence and interdependence in learning mathematics are nurtured by group work. Collaborating with peers gives students a chance to work out mathematical problems cooperatively. They are able to reason in nonthreatening situations, explore ideas together, experiment with various strategies, and concur on conclusions. Group members must explain and defend their partially formed ideas, while interpreting those of their peers and accepting alternative solutions. Best of all, they learn that they can help one another to succeed without having to rely on an external "expert."

Implementing student grouping requires active teacher participation. As children work in their groups, the teacher can move around the classroom to monitor progress by observing, listening, and asking questions. In so doing, he will become aware of which children most need content, language development, self-confidence, or group skills, and can tailor his directions, questioning, and interaction to best suit each child.

When children have not worked in groups previously, it might be best to start with pairs, rather than groups of three or four. Primary-grade children often work better with one partner than in larger groups and, in the beginning at least, cooperative habits might best be established in the smallest possible group combinations. When larger groups are necessary, some teachers assign roles—recorder, discussion leader, materials monitor, reporter. The teacher can foster independence by letting children know what is expected of them, thus enabling them to perform the appropriate tasks involved in their role. When tasks are rotated daily or weekly, each child has a chance to contribute in a variety of ways.

Collaborative activity demands that *all* members participate and progress, so although children have individual tasks to perform, they develop a sense of group responsibility. Groups must work together, making sure that each member understands the mathematics process involved. Rotating the role of group "presenter" requires that each member understand the process and actively participate, at least some of the time.

As with manipulatives, effective group work does not happen magically. It requires persistence and patience by teachers and students alike. Many teachers who successfully implement cooperative groups in their classrooms incorporate a common set of elements into their programs. They make sure to establish interesting and worthwhile tasks, activities, and problems for the groups to work on; they have a clearly defined set of classroom procedures that they stick to consistently and fairly; and they become active participants themselves, moving freely among the groups, entering into discussions, adding probing questions, and subtly facilitating the group process. Direct involvement provides them with opportunities for formative assessment of instructional effectiveness and student understanding.

Needless to say, as students become involved in tasks that they find interesting and understandable, the "busy noise" of activity is everywhere. Teachers, administrators, and classroom visitors need to be prepared for the sounds of *constructive noise* and understand that when children are working and talking in groups, the noise level will be higher than in a classroom in which children are more passive. Many teachers find it helpful to develop strategies that gain the attention of the whole group, perhaps by using hand signals or flicking the lights. Once students are accustomed to these strategies, they usually become quiet within a few seconds of the teacher's signal, especially if the ensuing discussion is interesting and allows for them to make their ideas known.

VALUING STUDENT-DEVELOPED PROCEDURES

"How did you do that—what was your thinking?" is a question often repeated in these classrooms. Teachers need to encourage students to develop their own procedures, and then provide supportive opportunities for children to verbalize their approaches. The NCTM standard on communication advocates this approach because as children verbalize their thinking, they define important components of the process they are explaining, sequence ideas, clarify procedures, and decide whether they are satisfied with their process and conclusion.

Children learn best when they actively build their own mathematical procedures and understandings, not when they simply sit back and receive information from the teacher or text. Reliance on teacher-prescribed algorithms does little to foster procedural understanding. When constructing their own knowledge, children develop strategies that they understand, believe in, can duplicate, and can explain through speaking and writing.

Many skills and understandings, particularly those associated with primary grades, can be developed by the students themselves if they

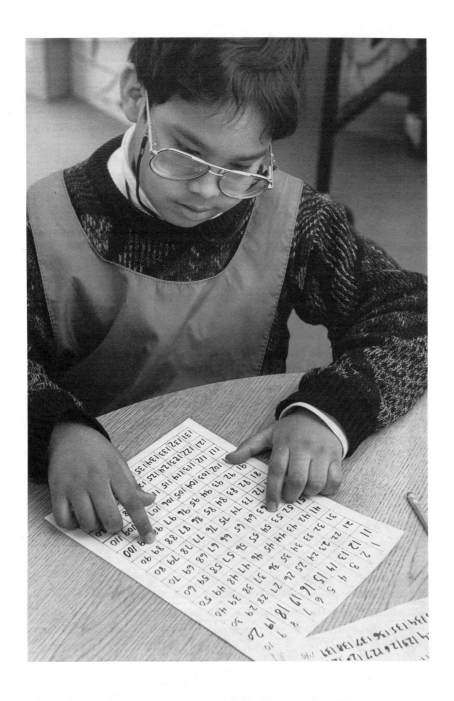

THINKING LIKE MATHEMATICIANS

are asked to solve meaningful problems. Developed in this way, these mathematics skills provide a strong foundation and lend a sense of ownership for the students.

Teachers can regularly ask children to explain their thinking. This is worthwhile for both "right" and "wrong" responses, as long as the teacher takes care not to make correctness seem the point of the exercise. Frequently, children will see where they went astray as they explain a procedure that got a "wrong" answer and will correct themselves in the process of their explanation.

When children explain their thinking to others, they personalize and concretize their own knowledge. Verbalizing one's thinking requires organization and understanding. It creates ownership of concepts. Often children arrive at a correct answer intuitively and are unaware of the specific mathematical procedures they applied. When they explain a solution, they are required to break that intuitive process into discrete steps and justify it. Their explanation, therefore, pushes them to develop a plan that they can use and modify each time they encounter a similar problem. In essence, they build their own algorithm. Sometimes, however, the explanation does not provide a replicable process by which to find a correct answer.

> *Kevin was given a story problem to solve about a girl at the fair. The problem was quite complicated for a second grader, and involved two rides, the number of tickets required for each ride, and the amount of time each ride lasted. Kevin needed to determine how many tickets the girl in the story would need if she wanted to ride each ride for six minutes. It took him very little time to solve the problem and give a correct answer.*
>
> *"How did you do that, Kevin?" asked his teacher. "What was your thinking?"*
>
> *Kevin launched into an explanation, but his explanation was faulty and was obviously leading him to a wrong answer. About halfway through his explanation, he stopped, realizing he was on the wrong track. He was stuck.*
>
> *The teacher remained silent. She did not make a suggestion. She did not call on another child to help get Kevin back on track. She did not even ask if he needed help. She simply waited and allowed him the time to think.*
>
> *After about thirty seconds, Kevin exclaimed, "Oh, now I know!" He started over and explained a logical procedure that produced the correct answer.*

As children explain their thinking—describe how they got a handle on a problem and solved it on their own—they are confirmed as mathematicians. They gain self-confidence. They are empowered to make their own decisions, find solutions, determine for themselves if they are right or wrong. As happened with Kevin, explaining an answer often helps children clarify a fuzzy idea about the method they used to reach a solution. Assured that their teacher values each idea, student mathematicians feel free to think creatively, and can then express their procedures openly. In turn, they learn to value the ideas of their classmates. If Kevin had not gotten on the right track after a reasonable wait time, his teacher might have allowed him to continue thinking while she went on to some other students, then she could have come back to him when he was ready.

Upon completion of a lesson in which children have solved problems individually or in small groups, it is productive to meet again in a whole-class format, allowing students the opportunity to share their procedures and ideas with the rest of the group. This not only provides closure for the lesson, it lets children listen to the wide variety of ways that any one problem can be solved. Students hear strategies that they may not have thought of on their own and, as they listen to their classmates, they must interpret and modify these other explanations in terms of their own constructs of understanding.

During these whole-class discussions, it is essential for *all* students to participate regularly. By repeatedly calling on only those who raise their hands, a teacher excludes the very students who most need to build confidence in their math, language, and social skills. In group discussions, usually the easiest concepts are contributed first. As an alternative to calling on hand-wavers, many teachers choose to connect first with those students weakest in their mathematics understanding or those who have difficulty communicating their ideas. Participating *first* allows these children to successfully contribute to group discussions, thus nurturing language and confidence in those students who may need this type of support. Additionally, this approach leaves the more complex concepts for the highly verbal and/or mathematically advanced students, and encourages them to stretch their own understanding and communication skills.

Teachers can prepare for the discussion by relating their observations of student work and students at work with the instructional goal of the activity, and then identifying strategies that will push the group closer to that goal. One technique for making the summary discussion more efficient and effective is to provide each group with a student slate or blank overhead transparency on which to record their strategies before the class discussion begins. All of the shared strategies can then be displayed simultaneously as the discussion takes place.

When children share their strategies, they are exposed to methodologies they may not have thought of. But this technique is not sufficient for building powerful learning experiences. The NCTM standards recommend that children not just *share* strategies, but *compare* them as well. Comparing one procedure with another allows children to generalize ideas, identify efficiency of procedures, and note processes that facilitate calculation and finding solutions: "How is Jen's method like Dean's?" "How is it different?" "Which one do you think would be easier for you to do?" "Which one took fewer steps?" "Which two strategies did you think were most alike?" "Which were most different?" "How would you write the numbers to show Anthony's strategy?"

USING THINKING STRATEGIES TO LEARN BASIC FACTS

Do you know the state capital of Wyoming, or the state bird? What is New Mexico's primary agricultural crop? These are not easy questions if you've forgotten your old geography facts. What can you do if you don't have the resources to look up the answers? Not much!

Now, what if you don't remember the sum of 3 + 4? How could you figure out the answer? Well, you could count on your fingers; or combine a group of three pencils with a group of four to represent the problem; or think of a fact that you do remember, such as 3 + 3, and add 1 to it. You might remember that 4 + 3 = 7, and realize that 3 + 4 must equal the same number. In other words, if you can use a variety of strategies to determine a basic number combination, it is not difficult to reconstruct a forgotten fact, or calculate a fact that has not previously been learned.

When children rote memorize basic number combinations as isolated facts, they have nothing to fall back on if they later forget one of those combinations. In the same way that committing fifty state capitals to memory contributes little to an understanding of government, the memorization of addition tables provides no understanding of math processes, no familiarity with addition concepts, and no safety net when memory fails. But children can develop basic strategies to help them discover answers for addition, subtraction, and even multiplication and division problems. Best of all, when they use these strategies in frequent and appropriate problem-solving situations, children eventually remember the facts naturally, without stress or fear of

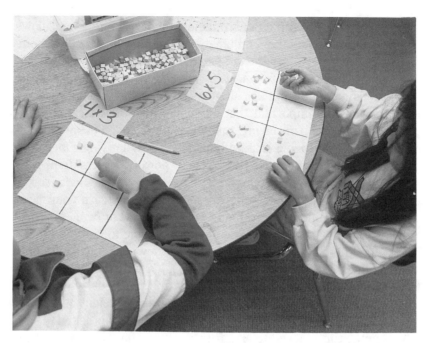

Children can be challenged to learn math facts in fun and meaningful ways.

failure. Research indicates that strategy-based learning of facts is much more efficient than rote recall of isolated answers (Thornton and Smith 1988; Fuson 1986).

Perhaps the most natural and frequently used strategy for learning and recalling basic number combinations for addition is "counting on." For example, when adding 8 + 3, the child starts at 8 and "counts on" three more—9, 10, 11. Although this strategy seems obvious, to many children it is not. Learning that they can always start with the larger number, whether it is on the right or the left, makes counting on even more powerful. Children realize that 3 + 8 is the same as 8 + 3. Knowing that they can "turn around" any addition combination is really using what mathematicians call the commutative property of addition. Just being able to count on by 1, 2, or 3 and knowing that any addition combination can be turned around enables children to find more than half of the basic facts for single-digit number combinations.

There are also certain fact patterns that children find easy to learn. "Doubles," such as 5 + 5 or 6 + 6, seem more easily learned than other number combinations. Using the more easily remembered facts and then coupling them with other strategies, such as counting on, allows children to figure out other combinations. A child who cannot remember the answer to 5 + 6, for example, may remember 5 + 5 = 10, and then count on one more to get 11.

There is no doubt that learning basic facts is essential to gaining math power. It is important that students know their facts and can apply them to problem-solving, mental arithmetic, and estimation situations. But memorizing facts without a means of deriving a forgotten fact robs students of control and the very power that lets them view themselves as mathematicians.

It is logical to ask, "What does it matter how you learn your facts, just as long as you do learn them?" *It is essential to know the basic facts.* Children who do not know them are unable to continue effectively with the mathematics learning, and they certainly can't apply their mathematics with accuracy. However, learning the facts without strategies to both recall forgotten facts and to check whether an answer is correct may, in the long run, be less efficient and much more prone to promote careless errors. When a child is asked to simply commit the answer to 8 + 5 to memory for later recall, the retrieved answer might be wrong. The child will not know it, and may repeatedly rehearse that wrong answer as she "practices" her addition tables. Once that wrong answer is firmly embedded in her memory, it is very difficult to erase and replace with the correct answer. On the other hand, if the answer is initially derived from known facts by using a strategy, then it is less likely to be wrong in the first place, and it can always be checked using strategies when it is next recalled. Children who know these strategies should be encouraged to "check" their answers, asking if they make sense.

Strategies are important and powerful tools for children to have when learning and recalling facts for addition and multiplication, but should never be taught to children as rules to memorize and use in certain ways or for particular digit combinations. To be truly effective, strategies must make sense and should be used flexibly when needed.

Students must continually be placed in situations in which they both need to know and have the means to determine simple facts. Over time, they will commit the facts to memory—naturally. Teachers can use a variety of methods to help children learn basic addition facts. Games that require adding the dots on a set of dice before moving a game piece are engaging and motivating. Such games should be based on random chance so that all students, not just the most capable, have an equal opportunity to win. Working with manipulatives often requires combining numbers to find totals. Combining sets of unifix cubes and adding and recording the numbers of sides on geometric pattern blocks are but two exercises that provide hands-on activity and plenty of repetition and practice. Classroom problems, such as those requiring students to determine the number of cookies needed for two tables of children, are real-world situations in which the combination of numbers has real purpose and, consequently, real meaning.

Ms. Valentine has found that fun fact activities can be connected with other curricular areas, especially art. One activity enables her to draw connections among math doubles, fractions, and symmetry (see Figure 7–2). Building on ideas from *Moving into Math* (Irons and Trafton 1992), she has the children fold paper to show two halves. (The halves can be as simple as torn squares, or as fancy as cut paper butterflies.) On one half, the children place a given number of dots of tempera paint. Then, quickly, before the paint can dry, they fold the dry half over onto the painted half.

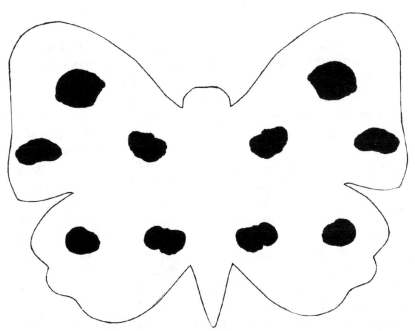

Figure 7–2 *Many interesting activities, such as this folded paper project, can be adapted to help children with math concepts.*

"Can you predict how many dots will show when the paper is unfolded?" Ms. Valentine asks the children. Having answered, they unfold, counting if necessary, and see if they were correct. Students keep their papers for reference and review of addition doubles. Sometimes, they add more dots in different colors or patterns (especially effective with folded butterflies) so they can then refer to the number of "pink dots," "yellow dots," or the total number of dots on the paper.

Ms. Valentine has even developed a means to use the painted dots for subtraction. She has the children count the total number of dots on the unfolded paper. Then they predict how many will be on one side. To check their prediction, they fold the paper and count the dots on one half.

Rather than helping children learn math with meaning, fact-based worksheets and timed drills contribute to math anxiety and can detract from a child's enjoyment of learning. Furthermore, when children complete these drills and worksheets without corrective feedback, they run the risk of memorizing incorrect math facts. It is essential that children take part in meaningful rather than repetitive activities that reinforce basic facts both in the classroom and at home. Parents are often willing to assist at home, but they should be encouraged to focus only on the facts their child is ready to learn next. Practice will be less stressful for children, especially when working with flashcards, if they are reminded to use strategies that help them figure out a fact they are having difficulty remembering. Challenging children to learn their math facts in ways that make sense to them enables students to develop strategies that will stay with them as they move into more complex and demanding mathematics procedures.

Allowing children to take responsibility for learning basic addition and multiplication facts can prove to be a powerful teaching strategy. One activity used by teachers following the NCTM standards recommendations uses blank addition fact tables. Students are first asked to fill in the facts that they know. Then they are asked how they can use the facts that they know to help them figure out some of the ones that they don't know. Students set goals and record their own progress. For example, children who know the facts for adding 3 to any number may use that as a stepping-stone to learn the facts for adding 4 to any number. ($5 + 3 = 8$, so $5 + 4 = 5 + 3 + 1 = 9$.) Children working on multiplication might choose to double the facts of 2 to learn the facts of 4, or to double the facts of 3 to learn the facts of 6. Making the choice of which facts to learn next and what strategy to use to learn these facts motivates children and asks them to "think like mathematicians."

IMPLEMENTING THE PROGRAM

Many teachers use one or two minutes each day to have children learn and then practice new strategies. At the beginning of math time, just before lining up for lunch, or at any other convenient time, they might ask, "If you couldn't recall the answer to $8 + 5$, what fact that you do recall could you use to help your memory?" Some children might break 5 down into $2 + 3$ and know that $8 + 2 = 10$, and then add 3 more to get 13. Some might break 8 into $3 + 5$ and then know that $3 + 5 + 5 = 13$ because they remember $5 + 5$. Still others might say that they remember $7 + 6 = 13$, and they can take 1 away from 8 and put it with 5 to make that combination. The same idea applies to multiplication facts. "If you couldn't recall the solution to 8×7, what strategies could you use to find it?" ($7 \times 7 = 49$ and add another 7; $8 \times 8 = 64$ and subtract a 7; $4 \times 7 = 28$ and then double 28; $10 \times 7 = 70$ and subtract 14.) Seeing that a forgotten fact can be retrieved in a variety of ways is empowering.

Subtraction facts are probably best learned by connecting them with addition facts. These can be learned as fact "families." ($7 + 5 = 12$, $5 + 7 = 12$, $12 - 7 = 5$, and $12 - 5 = 7$ is the fact family of 7, 5, and 12.) Using addition strategies to learn the addition facts and then connecting the subtraction facts to them builds a powerful tool for recalling subtraction facts and reinforces the important connection between addition and subtraction.

It is probably a waste of instructional time to have children learn or be tested on division facts. They are almost never used. Think about how division is done, whether by the traditional algorithm or a procedure invented by a student. First of all, most division problems in real life have remainders. Dividing 78 by 8 cannot be done easily by using a fact. We usually say that 8×9 is 72, and there is a remainder of 6. Some may see that 8×10 is 80, so the answer is 9 with a remainder of $8 - 2$ or 6. In either case, it is the multiplication fact that is used. Multiplication facts are the powerful and strategic tools that are used most effectively for dividing.

Some of the fact strategies that are powerful and appropriate for initial learning or recalling a forgotten fact include the following:

ADDITION AND SUBTRACTION

Counting on	1, 2, 3
Turning a fact around	$3 + 8 = 8 + 3$ (addition and multiplication only)
Doubles	$8 + 8 = 16$
	$16 - 8 = 8$

Doubles + 1	$7 + 8 = 7 + 7 + 1$
Sum of 10	$6 + 4 = 10$
Near doubles (or compensation)	$8 + 6 = (8 - 1) + (6 + 1) = 7 + 7$

MULTIPLICATION

Relate to repeated addition	$4 \times 3 = 3 + 3 + 3 + 3$
Visualize as an array	□ □ □ □ □ □
	□ □ □ □ □ □
Facts of 2 and 5	$2, 4, 6, 8, 10 \ldots$
by skip counting	$5, 10, 15, 20 \ldots$
Turning a fact around	$7 \times 4 = 4 \times 7$
Learning the concept, "1 x any number is that number"	$1 \times 7 = 7$
Learning the concept "0 x any number is 0"	$0 \times 7 = 0$
Building facts of 3 on those of 2	$3 \times 4 = (2 \times 4) + 4$
Building facts of 4 by doubling those of 2	$4 \times 6 = (2 \times 6) \times 2$
Building facts of 6 on those of 5	$6 \times 3 = (5 \times 3) + 3$
Building facts of 6 by doubling those of 3	$6 \times 7 = (3 \times 7) \times 2$
Building facts of 4 on those of 5	$4 \times 7 = (5 \times 7) - 7$
Seeing a pattern in the facts for 9 (there are many)	Sum of the digits in the products always equals 9. Tens digits increase by 1 as the ones digits decrease by 1 (45, 54, 63, 72).

ENCOUNTERING MATH THROUGHOUT THE CURRICULUM

It almost goes without saying that in order to encourage children to value mathematics, they must see that it is useful in their personal lives and throughout the curriculum, all through the day. Math talk should be standard for students' complete language development, not just for one-hour math class each morning. Math principles must provide the foundation for collecting, recording, and interpreting information from the other content areas.

Daily routines are rife with math potential. Many teachers like to

Using a Venn diagram for attendance creates opportunities for class discussion.

use attendance each morning to reinforce mathematics. Students can place magnetic name tags or Post-it notes on a graph or a Venn diagram when they enter the room in the morning. Those not placing their marker (after a reminder, if necessary) are the students who are absent. A Venn diagram for attendance could use the statements, "I took a bus to school," "I rode in a car," "I walked to school," to require children to make complex decisions about where to place their marker if, for example, their dad gave them a ride to the bus stop.

Teachers who look for opportunities to use math throughout the day find that there is no subject that cannot be incorporated into, or

THINKING LIKE MATHEMATICIANS

benefit from, mathematics: weighing, measuring, recording, and interpreting science data; graphing statistics gathered in social studies; preparing and distributing art materials; or measuring distances or recording statistics in physical education activities. Every curricular area benefits from mathematical exploration.

EVALUATION

Dr. William Smith, the local math supervisor, was observing Ms. Lorraine Howard's second-grade class. When he arrived, the children were just completing a "favorite flavor graph" that charted several flavors of ice cream and each child's favorite. Anxious to highlight the good thinking that was going on in her class, Ms. Howard said to the children, "Look at the graph and tell me something you see up there." Immediately, several hands went up in the air.

"Most kids like chocolate the best," said one girl.

"Who can tell me something different?" the teacher asked.

"Nobody likes banana flavor," said a boy.

"Toni and I were the only ones who liked orange sherbet. More people liked vanilla," another child observed.

"Great. Can anyone tell me something different?" persisted Ms. Howard, trying to ferret out every idea.

"I see a pattern the way people like the flavors," ventured another boy.

"Tell us your pattern, Jeffrey," responded Ms. Howard.

Jeffrey proceeded to give a literal description of the graph: "Two kids like orange sherbet, lots liked chocolate, but Charise was the only one who liked bubble gum. Me, Anthony, Jon, and Adelle like cookie dough. That's four. And nobody liked banana and three liked vanilla." His answer appeared to tell nothing about patterns. Ms. Howard did not see a pattern in Jeffrey's response and she felt bad for him that he demonstrated such a lack of understanding before the visitor, but Dr. Smith's enthusiasm was undampened.

"That's great information!" he exclaimed. "Look at what we've learned about that child that may also apply to others in the group. He knows the word pattern and he wants to use it, but he needs help in understanding it. You can use that information to plan an activity with patterns to help you see if other students have the same needs and to help Jeffrey and others get a better understanding of patterns."

They went on to discuss ways that Ms. Howard could help Jeffrey build his understanding of patterns. He needed activities in which he extended existing patterns before creating patterns on his own. Ms. Howard decided she would have Jeffrey and his classmates sort patterns from nonpatterns and then have them explain how they decided which were which. That way, she would know if they truly understood what constitutes patterns. Because children sometimes see patterns where adults do not, Dr. Smith agreed, it is important to always ask them to explain their thinking as they do the activity.

This story underscores a central theme in new approaches to assessment. Assessment can take place at any time, in any situation; it is often more accurate when noted in nontest situations; and, most important, it is an essential tool for guiding the direction of instruction. Evaluation can be a formative process, one that determines where children's strengths and weaknesses are. As such, it should be used not only to guide instruction, but also as a tool to assess the strengths and weaknesses of the instructional process itself.

Assessment goes hand in hand with instruction, so when instructional practices change, the forms of assessment and evaluation must complement the instructional practices. To this end, the NCTM standards place strong emphasis on evaluation practices. One of the six fundamental principles is the assessment principle:

> Assessment should support the learning of important mathematics and furnish useful information to both teachers and students. (*Principles and Standards*, 22)

Assessment in traditional instruction has most often focused on evaluation and grading. Those are legitimate uses of assessment, but using it to help shape instructional plans is even more important. The NCTM standards stress the fact that good assessment used well can "enhance students' learning." The following summarizes some of the important ideas about assessment that are found in the standards documents:

- Assessment should reflect the mathematics that all students need to know and be able to do.
- Overreliance on formal assessments may give an incomplete and perhaps distorted picture of student performance.
- Because different students show what they know and can do in different ways, assessments should allow for multiple approaches, thus giving a well-rounded picture and allowing each student to show his or her greatest strengths.

- When teachers are selecting assessment methods, the age, experience, and special needs of students should be considered.
- When done well, assessment that is used to gather information for instructional planning can also be used to judge student attainment.
- Assessment should always be an equitable process.
- Assessment should be an open process.

The *Principles and Standards* states:

> To ensure deep, high-quality learning for all students, assessment and instruction must be integrated so that assessment becomes a routine part of the ongoing classroom activity rather than an interruption. Such assessment also provides the information teachers need to make appropriate instructional decisions. In addition to formal assessments, such as tests and quizzes, teachers should be continually gathering information about their students' progress through informal means, such as asking questions during the course of a lesson, conducting interviews with individual students, and giving writing prompts. (23)

> Many assessment techniques can be used by mathematics teachers, including open-ended questions, constructed-response tasks, selected-response items, performance tasks, observations, conversations, journals, and portfolios. (23)

It's clear that the diversity of instructional practices recommended by the NCTM standards documents is accompanied by an equal diversity in recommended forms of assessment. They can be implemented individually or in small or large groups. Evaluation can be presented in many ways: oral, written, demonstration, or even computer-based formats. Appropriate assessment instruments include (but are not restricted to) discussion, written tasks, journals, homework, special projects, and class presentations. "Simply put," states the *Curriculum and Evaluation Standards*, "assessment should not rely on a single instrument or technique" (192).

Standardized tests have long been a staple of American schools, but many educators know the downside of large-scale, norm-referenced tests. These tests don't always indicate the student's mathematical progress, reasoning ability, or conceptual understanding, but merely record the ability to provide the correct answer to a specific problem on a given day. Usually, standardized tests indicate what students do not know, rather than revealing what they do know. Placing undo emphasis on tests leads administrators, parents, and the public at large to focus on the results of the assessment itself, when they could be focusing on the true understanding of the mathematical concepts the tests set out to evaluate.

It goes without saying, however, that there must be some form of accountability for instructional practice. Parents have the right to feel confident that their children are learning the concepts and facts that will enable them to succeed in the future; administrators must justify school procedures to parents and taxpayers; and teachers need to know that their methods of instruction are helping every child learn and grow mathematically. Many teachers are using methods, both formal and informal, that address these needs and at the same time more effectively assess the mathematical understanding of individual children. The standards documents strongly recommend that any assessments, whether administered for accountability or instructional decision making, should have adequate variety to ensure that all children have the opportunity to demonstrate what they know about the mathematics. In the primary grades one of the best methods to gather information for both purposes is simply to ask questions that have children express their thinking and then to listen and observe carefully.

INFORMAL ASSESSMENT

Informal assessment presents student progress in relation to the instructional content, often over time as students mature developmentally and progress mathematically. Informal assessment is characterized by its open-ended format and individualized nature, which allows it to be tailored to the needs of each teacher and each student. Perhaps best of all, this mode of assessment does not take time away from the instructional process. Rather, it can be incorporated into the math program, can benefit student instruction, and can help identify needed change in the instructional process.

There are many ways teachers informally evaluate students, for in a child-centered classroom almost everything a teacher does is aimed at knowing more about the students and what they are doing. Three specific methods, anecdotal records, student portfolios, and student journals, are representative of informal assessment strategies that can be incorporated into mathematics programs at the primary-grade level.

Anecdotal Records

Teach-and-test methods of evaluation only assess percentages of correct (or incorrect) answers for a specific task, but anecdotal records provide a means to record student levels of thinking, reasoning, problem solving, and communicating mathematically. When compiled over time—a month, a year, or an entire elementary school career—they provide a lens through which to view students' development and progress. When keeping anecdotal records, teachers are able to evaluate the concept development behind the answers, record which strategies seem to work best for a student, and pinpoint specific misconceptions that repeatedly interfere with conceptual understanding.

In classrooms where children are encouraged to construct their own understanding, every child is actively involved in math processes—investigating and acting on objects, describing those actions and results, sharing ideas with peers and adults, explaining thinking, and justifying solutions. Such classroom scenarios are rife with opportunities for teachers to observe, listen to, and record student thinking. Brief notes about student ideas, insights, and misconceptions provide glimpses of a child's thinking. As with portraits in a photo album, no one "picture" represents a child's total mathematical "history" and awareness. But when compiled over time, these pictures draw a more complete portrait of the child: her strengths, weaknesses, thinking style, and conceptual awareness—where she stands mathematically.

When children work in pairs or small groups, each child has a chance to participate actively and has a forum for discussion, negotiation, and the give and take of mathematical ideas common to group activity. Cooperative grouping facilitates anecdotal record keeping because it gives the teacher a chance to move about the room, observe student activity, and listen to each child. How else can she discover what each child is thinking?

Paired activity can be applied in almost any math situation. For example, when exploring the "favorite flavor graph," Ms. Howard might have begun by saying to the students, "Think about the graph for a minute. Now turn to the person next to you and tell that person something you noticed about the graph." With a single question, every child would be thinking, and then sharing, his or her ideas. At the same time, Ms. Howard would have had the opportunity to walk around the room and listen to the children's comments. Conversations that indicated specific misconceptions or good insight could have been recorded for notation in the child's record. The process could then have continued in the group discussion when many different ideas were explored.

Ms. Howard would not want to record every comment she heard, but certainly some would stand out as unusual, and therefore important for her records. She might note that, like Jeffrey, several children seem to have a misunderstanding of patterns. The comments of other students might indicate an advanced concept development, perhaps an understanding of subtraction processes or facts.

While monitoring students at work or in discussion, teachers should ask questions that cause students to describe their thinking. "How do you know that is the least popular choice?" "What is the next least popular choice? How do you know that?" "How did you decide on what you wanted to share?" Asking children to share one observation paves the way for contributing one idea, but following this up by asking, "Who sees something different?" encourages students to look at the situation from many new perspectives. This emphasis on different perspectives would have allowed Ms. Howard to assess the highest level of student thinking rather than the simplest and most obvious answers. Students must stretch their minds and use higher-level thinking skills to view a problem from many angles.

In order to ensure that no child is falling through the cracks, many teachers select a different set of students to monitor with each instructional activity. Over a period of seven or eight days they will have accrued notes on every student. There may be children who need more frequent observation, either because they are struggling or because they have shown some unusual thinking that indicates the need for greater challenge.

Teachers who make the rounds of the classroom while children are engaged in math activities, or who guide a whole-group discussion in which children explain their thinking, are in the perfect position to make anecdotal records about each and every child in their class. This need not become a burdensome task. Few teachers make these notations all the time, even when something notable occurs. Rather, they designate specific activities as record-keeping opportunities—for example, those that involve students wrestling with a particularly important concept, such as place value.

Many teachers develop strategies that help them take notes more effectively and efficiently. For example, some teachers use "sticky" notes or labels as a quick way to record selective comments about student performance. Later they adhere them to student folders and then review them periodically to make sure no children are overlooked. Other teachers use loose-leaf notebooks with sections designated by student or subject and add pages as necessary. Many take advantage of instructional assistants, parent volunteers, or student teachers to take notes on students. However, because this deprives the teacher of direct observation, it might be more beneficial to have the assistant lead an activity while the teacher makes notes like those shown in Figure 8–1 on p. 108.

Portfolios

Mathematics portfolios provide a means to collect a representative sampling of student work over a period of time. They provide data with which to assess student progress over the year and to communicate that progress with parents, administrators, and the students themselves.

Because it is impractical to collect all student work, teachers must develop their own criteria for selecting the portfolio contents. For example, the teacher and the student can each choose one item to represent a week's work. Sometimes the teacher even encourages parents to choose a paper for their child's portfolio.

The child will probably decide to include the work she feels best about, and the parents, if they choose to contribute, will most likely pick a paper that they feel highlights the child's strengths. But there is some debate over which papers the teacher should choose. The general purpose of the portfolio is to show a sampling of work indicative of student achievement. But should the paper be the student's best work of that week, or work that is simply representative of her general performance? Obviously, this is the teacher's decision and must be based on his personal teaching philosophy and what he knows about his students.

However, there are strong arguments in favor of consistently including the best work from any student. No teacher will ever know with certainty that what he believes is typical of a child's performance actually represents what the child understands and can do. By consistently including a child's best work, he records what the child ultimately is capable of doing, and probably what she really understands. Additionally, a child's best work provides a basis for making appropriately challenging plans for upcoming instruction. In any case, whatever the decision, the criteria for selection should probably be noted in the portfolio.

At first glance, portfolio collections seem restricted to pencil-and-paper tasks. In fact, although their contents are limited to tangible forms, portfolios can include a variety of recorded materials. Photos can be taken of projects that cannot be included—group work, outdoor projects, a student-constructed bulletin board display. Students

Figure 8–1 *Many teachers keep index cards with them as they observe and work with children. Separate cards can be filed under each child's name in a file box. It's fairly easy to update information on the cards.*

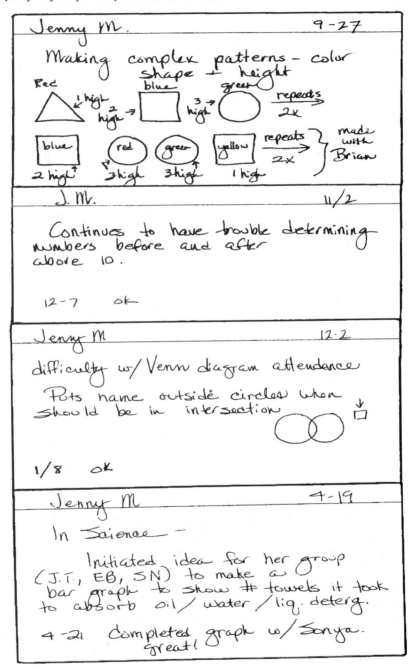

Problem #2 Four children want to share nine apples so that everyone gets the same amount. How many apples would each child get?

I solved the problem by giving each child 2 apples. Then I had 1 apple left so then I cut the apple into fourths. Then everybody ended up with 2 + a 1/4.

Figure 8–2 *A variety of work samples that demonstrate multiple strategies for solving problems should be included in a child's portfolio.*

can create data collection records, narrative descriptions, pencil tracings, crayon rubbings, or illustrations of hands-on activities and classroom experiences in which they were involved. In the primary grades particularly, an adult may record a child's oral description of his or her thinking that the child would not have been able to record (see Figure 8–2). What's more, besides providing a record for students' files, alternative recording activities have instructional benefit. Graphic representation, such as writing, drawing, or charting, provides closure and helps to concretize the abstract ideas children have after hands-on experiences.

Reviewing portfolios helps teachers document the mathematical progress of individual students and the class as a whole. But students, too, can benefit from their collected work when encouraged to review, assess, and reflect on their progress. Teachers can even create instructional activities that encourage personal reflection. An activity calling for personal reflection in math might incorporate writing and integrate other subjects. For example, in May, second graders might look at a science measurement activity they did in September and compare it with one they did in February. What did they do differently in February than they did in September? Was it more efficient? What do they know now that they didn't even know in February? How would the student teach that early September lesson to an incoming second grader next year?

Portfolios are student-specific assessment tools that document program content and student progress. When kept over the course of several grades, they indicate student strengths and development from year to year. Student portfolios provide a means of assessing where a student currently is in terms of his math understanding, how he is progressing, which modalities of communication appeal most to his individual strengths, and, perhaps most telling, what he thinks is his best work.

The contents of one student's portfolio might include:

- an answer to an open-ended math question
- a description or photo of a group project
- an individual math project
- a math-related science project, such as collecting and recording weather data
- graphs done for social studies
- math-related work from another subject area
- story problems created by the student
- drawings done for math
- copies of interesting journal entries
- teacher anecdotes
- papers on which the student has corrected errors
- work done outside of school for math
- a math poster design

Student Journals

Student journals need not fall under the exclusive domain of the language arts curriculum. As many teachers are discovering, science, social studies, and even mathematics learning can benefit from personal reflection through journal writing.

Writing mathematical ideas serves much the same function as verbally discussing these ideas. It concretizes thinking. It helps forge connections among mathematics concepts. It demands that students break down abstract and intuitive conclusions into logical, sequential, and often replicable processes. And it allows students to do this in a nonrestrictive and nonjudgmental format. The journal is theirs. It is personal. They alone decide what they will write in it. Because chil-

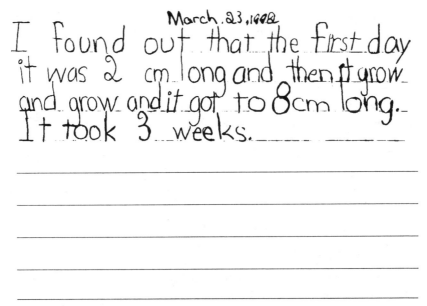

March. 23, 1998

I found out that the first day
it was 2 cm long and then it grow
and grow and it got to 8cm long.
It took 3 weeks.

Figure 8–3 Journal writing allows children to record events, observations, and ideas.

dren know that their entries will not be corrected, graded, or judged, they feel free to express their true thinking, not just the words they think the teacher will approve of. Consequently, journals like that shown in Figure 8–3 offer a window into students' understanding.

Mathematics journal writing in the elementary grades can involve drawing pictures, writing equations, developing story problems, or discussing reactions to a math activity. Math journals can be graphic, numeric, or narrative. Usually, math journals at these grade levels are responses to teacher-generated journal prompts. These can be tailored to demonstrate understanding of specific concepts the teacher is assessing, but should always be open ended. In kindergarten and first grade, class journals can be done using a language experience approach. The teacher can elicit (and assess) ideas from the children during a group discussion and record those ideas on chart paper. The pages can be kept throughout the year on an easel and/or copied into a smaller format for later reference.

Journal prompts (like those in Figure 8–4) must be developmentally appropriate. The youngest children, those in kindergarten or just entering first grade, might be asked to draw a picture that shows six, or

Figure 8–4

Each prompt must be tailored to suit the needs of a specific teacher, group of students, and particular learning task. Some sample prompts taken from a variety of classes include:

- Show three different drawings for the number five (5).
- Write three story problems that have five (5) as an answer.
- Write about your favorite number. Tell why it is your favorite.
- Make up a pattern and tell about it.
- Find out how many windows are in your home. Tell how you did this.
- Write three story problems for the picture on page 45 of your book. Tell how to solve the problems.
- Find out the favorite ice cream flavor for ten people you know. Invent a way to show this information to your class.
- Spin this spinner ten times. Tell what happened. Tell why you think it happened.
- What was easiest (hardest) for you in today's math lesson? Why?
- What did you like most in math this week? Why?
- Write ten problems that use the number 10.
- Try to solve these problems mentally (no paper, pencil, or calculator). Write how you solved them.
- Write how you would tell a younger child to do the work we learned in math today.
- Make up ten math problems that you think are easy to do without paper, pencil, or calculator. Tell why you think they are easy.

that illustrates what the children did during a mathematics activity. More mature students can be expected to use appropriate number symbols and narrative style. Prompts might require that students write five "number sentences" that use the number 10, or describe a sphere without drawing a picture. Or students could be asked to respond to specific questions whose answers will provide special insight into their individual mathematical struggles, aptitudes, and attitudes.

Journal prompts can help a teacher assess the breadth of her students' grasp of concepts. For example, when trying to determine whether children recognize subtraction in more than just its "take away" form, a teacher might offer the following prompts on three consecutive days:

1. Josh had 8 stickers and he gave 3 to Maria. How many stickers does Josh have now? How would you solve this? Why do you think that works?

2. The basket had 13 apples and oranges. There were 5 apples. How many oranges were there? How would you solve this? Why do you think that works?
3. Darian had 11 stickers. Juan had 17 stickers. How many more stickers did Juan have than Darian? How would you solve this? Why do you think that works?

Reviewing student responses will allow teachers to see where each child is individually, and whether the class as a whole understands the types and breadth of situations where subtraction can be used to solve problems.

Perhaps as clearly as any other assessment tool, student journals can serve the dual purposes of assessment and instruction. Joan Countryman, in her book *Writing to Learn Mathematics* (1992), explains why writing helps mathematics learning: "Writing strengthens a student's experience of a new concept. Students get immediate feedback from the words that they produce. When students write, they are integrating the work of the hand, the eye, and the brain. They fix on the page connections and relationships between what they already know and what they are meeting for the first time" (10). Later she explains why she values journal writing for her mathematics students: "Reading math journal entries tells me considerably more about what students grasp and do not understand, like and dislike, care about and reject as they study mathematics than any formal or traditional math assignments. I find myself more aware of what students know, and how they come to construct that knowledge" (28–29).

A note of caution: As a general rule, the expected levels of writing should be low enough that they do not interfere with mathematics assessment. Writing is difficult for some children and may not provide an accurate picture of a child's mathematical understanding. All students, especially those who are not fluent writers, can benefit from modifications to the writing tasks. For example, students can occasionally dictate to adults, draw pictures to represent their ideas, or select from a variety of preprinted responses.

FORMAL ASSESSMENT

Using a variety of open-ended, informal assessment techniques gives a comprehensive picture of the instructional needs of individual students and the class as a whole. However, sometimes teachers, administrators, and parents feel more formal assessments are needed.

Formal assessments are usually a set of questions or tasks given to all students in a consistent and replicable manner. They do not necessarily have to result in a grade, but they do include evaluation of student mastery of specific concepts.

There are several reasons why teachers, or the school administration, may decide that formal assessments are worthwhile. Formal assessments can help to:

- indicate whether the program is moving along in a consistent and productive manner;
- provide an effective means to communicate with parents and administrators;
- validate informal observations that the teacher has made about the students; and
- offer some level of consistent information about all students.

Sometimes, the results of the formal assessment are inconsistent with those of the informal assessments about a particular child. This suggests that the child's progress needs to be verified. Usually, it is the informal assessments that provide the most reliable data about a child's understanding. Inconsistencies in results might simply indicate that the child does not perform well in formal assessment situations, or that he was having a "bad day."

Many school districts impose an array of formal assessment instruments on teachers and students. The classroom teacher often has little control over their inclusion in the school program. Although teachers may supplement large-scale formal tests with their own less formal, but often more informative (and reliable) assessment methods, it is mandated formal assessments that receive the most public exposure and administrative scrutiny. Standardized, norm-referenced tests do not always document accurate levels of understanding and achievement for many children. But because the results of these tests are public and often political, teachers are often encouraged, even pressured, into "teaching to the test." This type of teaching does not provide students with the kind of instruction that enables them to be independent solvers of problems, to "think like mathematicians," and therefore does not reflect the recommendations of the NCTM standards documents. In fact, test results from schools involved in the project reported on in this book clearly demonstrate that students who are taught to think and problem solve, rather than spend instructional time learning test-driven skills and content, do very well on multiple-choice tests.

Student Interviews

Individual student interviews may or may not be considered formal testing. Though time-consuming in a busy classroom environment, individual student interviews can provide sufficiently valuable and different information to justify their occasional use. It is beneficial for a teacher to meet with each student individually once, perhaps twice, during the course of the year, to assess some aspects of mathematical progress. A teacher may decide that the interview is particularly helpful for a student about whom she is having difficulty getting adequate information through other means. This may be a student who is not a native speaker of English, or a student whose errors in a particular concept don't seem to fall into an explainable pattern. Such interviews aren't informal conversations, but rather a planned set of tasks and questions that provide insight into a student's understanding of specific concepts. These interviews can be accomplished while the rest of the children are working independently or when another adult is working with them.

If, for example, a teacher wanted to determine how well her students understood place value, she could develop an appropriate question, set out a variety of materials (base-ten blocks, multilink cubes, or beans), and ask each child to solve the problem using any strategy he wanted. He could use the materials, draw a picture, or write the problem out numerically on paper, but he would need to explain what he did and why. By carefully designing four or five problems that address specific content areas, teachers can generate a picture of each student's mathematical development on that set of mathematical concepts. By requiring the same tasks of everyone, teachers can evaluate the progress of the class as a whole and any one student's relative standing within the class.

One set of questions for second graders might include the following prompts. Props for this task include four cards—one for each numeral—1, 2, 3, and 4; and patterns for double-digit addition and subtraction (marked boxes to place each card).

Prompt One: Here are four digits on cards (1, 2, 3, 4). Here is a pattern for an addition problem. Arrange these cards on the pattern to make two 2-digit numbers that, when added together, will equal the largest possible sum.

Figure 8–5

Prompt Two: Here is a different pattern, this time for a subtraction problem. Use the cards to make a subtraction problem whose answer is the biggest possible number.

2.   □   □
   –   □   □
   _____

Figure 8–6

These questions give insight into understandings of place value and the effect of the operations of addition and subtraction. If the student responds correctly, he could go on to solve an additional problem that used different digits, or the goal could be changed to the smallest possible sum and the smallest possible difference. If he answers incorrectly, then the follow-up might be for the student simply to arrange two or three of the digits to make the greatest number he can. If, after each response, students are asked to explain their thinking, some students may be able to correct their errors.

Individual assessments may provide surprising insights into student understanding and can be used to guide instruction. Consider this fourth grader's response to a single interview question:

Ellis was given the following problem:

"Four children had three bags of M&M candies. They decided to open all three bags and share the candies fairly. There were 52 candies in each bag. How many candies did each child get?"

Ellis thought for a moment and then launched into his response (see Figure 8–7).

"Well, first I did this: I said three times fifty-two is, three times fifty-two is a hundred fifty, fifty-two, fifty-four, fifty-six. Three times fifty-two is a hundred fifty-six.

"Then I did this: I numbered the four children [writes 1, 2, 3, 4 and draws vertical lines separating the numbers].

"Then I said twenty, forty, sixty, eighty [writes a 20 below each of the numbers 1, 2, 3, and 4].

"Then I said: [pauses] eighty-five, ninety, ninety-five, one hundred [writes a 5 below each of the 20s].

"Then I said: a hundred ten, hundred twenty, hundred thirty, hundred forty [writes a 1 below each of the 5s]. Oops, these are tens [puts a 0 behind each 1].

"Hundred forty-one, forty-two, forty-three, forty-four . . . hundred fifty-six [writes 1s in the columns below the 10s until he gets to his target of 156].

Figure 8–7

"The answer is twenty, twenty-five, thirty-five, thirty-six, thirty-seven, thirty-eight, thirty-nine.

"The answer is thirty-nine."

Ellis is a fourth-grade student who had never been taught a formal procedure for division. But he was used to inventing his own ways of solving problems and was in the habit of sharing his thought processes. He was able, therefore, to tackle this difficult problem. Seeing this basic understanding of division on the part of several of her students enabled Ellis's teacher to build on the existing knowledge so that teaching and learning would be more efficiently accomplished. Wouldn't it be great if all students could attack two-step problems with the confidence and enthusiasm that Ellis showed? Maybe they can. Having students develop confidence and make sense of the mathematics they use is a major goal of the National Council of Teachers of Mathematics with its standards documents.

No single assessment method gives a total picture of a child's mathematical achievement or understanding. Each provides just a glimpse of the child at any one point in time. But like the combined pieces of a jigsaw puzzle, an array of assessments forms a reasonable, cohesive picture. Teachers should have as much control as possible over the assessment that is used. When assessments are teacher-developed or teacher-selected, they can be more specifically matched to the needs of individual students or the class as a whole. They provide feedback that the teacher can reflect on and use to modify instructional plans. They also are better matched to, and indicative of, the teacher's instructional strategies. Furthermore, assessments that meet the needs of the students and match the instructional strategies of the teacher can provide a better indication of the general progress of the teacher's mathematics program.

9
••••••
THE CASE OF ONE YOUNG
MATHEMATICIAN

*T*yrone *was handed the following card and was asked to solve the problem and explain his thinking.*

$$41 - 29 = \underline{\qquad}$$

He proceeded with confidence. "First I should make this a 30," he said, pointing to the 29. "So I'll add one on. Later on I'll take it away. So you have 41 take away 30. That's 11, and then you take away the 1. That's 12."

What an interesting procedure for a second grader to create! But as reasonable as it is, it is a far cry from the traditional subtraction algorithm that is taught and required of most second-grade children. One wonders how successfully Tyrone would perform in a class that requires students always to solve problems in the traditional manner. It is fortunate for Tyrone that he experienced his first- and second-grade years in classrooms that valued student-created procedures as much as the solutions that were found.

Tyrone's nontraditional method of solving this subtraction problem did not obey the conventional rules taught for double-digit subtraction with regrouping. Yet it is a quick, efficient, and effective solution *for Tyrone*. It indicates an understanding of numbers and their relationships in the subtraction process. And it exemplifies the thought processes of a budding young mathematician.

Tyrone is a child with unusual math potential. He is thoughtful and highly verbal. His thinking is creative and unique, and demonstrates a well-developed insight into mathematical concepts. But Tyrone is very quiet, and despite his strong verbal capabilities and his obvious mathematical skills, he does not stand out in his class. Tyrone could be passed over as simply another child of average ability. His uncommon approaches to solving math problems might even fool a teacher into believing Tyrone didn't grasp a concept. Add to this situation the fact that Tyrone attends a school that generally has low scores on standardized tests and therefore has low expectations placed on its students, Tyrone's mathematical future might be bleak.

What if Tyrone were not in a math program that encouraged him to explain his thinking? If he were just told to use the traditional way of solving the problem, would he have concluded that his own thinking was wrong and should not be used? He might even have had difficulty understanding the traditional way because it does not match his thinking. Its logic does not match the number sense that he demonstrated. What might this have done to his confidence? It is impossible to know, but in any event, it is much less likely that he would have continued to build with his own way of thinking. It is also less likely that he would have emerged from the primary grades ready to think like a mathematician.

As with any mathematician, math is not always easy for Tyrone. Often he must wrestle with, and return to, a problem that he has difficulty solving, but his tenacity usually enables him to find a satisfying and creative solution. As a first grader, Tyrone had been given the problem $42 - 25 =$ _____. He wrote down 21 in the space provided, but seemed uncertain about his answer. Although he could have stopped at that point, he decided to try again. He copied the problem vertically, but placed the 25 above the 42.

$$\begin{array}{r} 25 \\ -\,42 \\ \hline \end{array}$$

He subtracted the 2 from the 5 in the ones column and then stopped. He realized that he could not take the 4 from the 2.

Noting his perplexed look, his teacher asked whether he would like to use some base-ten blocks. Tyrone reached over and counted out four tens and two ones to represent the 42. To subtract the 25, he removed two of the tens and then counted up five places on one of the remaining tens. Using his finger to mark that spot, he counted what remained. "The answer is seventeen," he said, but with a tone of uncertainty. He looked back at the paper and said, "Let me look at this again." Then he rewrote the problem, this time placing the 42 on top, but got an answer of 23.

He noted that he now had three different answers: 21, 17, and 23. "Which one is right?" he asked.

The teacher turned it back to him. "Which do *you* think?"

"I think the blocks," he said hesitantly. "So I think the answer is seventeen."

The teacher had him write down his answer and she prepared to move on. But Tyrone was still not ready to let go. "Seventeen, plus twenty-five is . . . What is seventeen plus twenty-five?" he asked aloud, as though still trying to remove his doubt. Without wasting a moment, Tyrone practically crawled across the table to grab the blocks back. He counted, this time taking a very sophisticated approach, "seventeen, twenty-seven, thirty-seven, thirty-eight, thirty-nine, forty, forty-one, forty-two. The answer was seventeen!" he said with certainty and great enthusiasm. And with the problem resolved, he was finally able to move on.

This was not a simple problem for a child Tyrone's age, and several times during this task the teacher gave him a chance to go on to the next problem. At least once, she started to pack up the materials, but Tyrone was not about to let this problem go unsolved. He had obtained three different answers. He knew this couldn't be, and he was obviously unsure of his pencil-and-paper arithmetic. Concrete materials gave Tyrone the means to discover the answer in a way he could see and understand, check his answer, and resolve the conflict left by the paper-and-pencil procedures.

At this point, Tyrone was ready to record the work he was doing with the base-ten blocks and make a direct connection between what he now believed to be a correct process and a pencil-and-paper record of it. That would give him an algorithm he understood. Later, he would be able to move to a more efficient (and perhaps traditional) algorithm if that proved useful to him.

It's highly probable that if Tyrone had been given similar problems on a worksheet and was not provided the time for reflection or the hands-on materials to support his work, he would have gotten many answers wrong. He would have learned nothing in the process; his teacher would not have seen his ability to stick with a problem or his capacity to solve it; and most important, he would not have gained the confidence that accompanies constructing a solution and then validating it. Tyrone would not have had the opportunity to connect his insightful work with blocks to a pencil-and-paper procedure.

Encouraging children to communicate their mathematical thinking reveals many student capabilities that would go unnoticed in a program that looks only for right or wrong answers. When children are given the tools and encouragement to convince themselves that they have gotten a correct solution, they gain an inner confidence that cannot be derived by having a teacher judge their work. Like Tyrone, they become mathematically empowered.

Sometimes Tyrone's explanations can be long and involved, and even confusing to the observer, but they usually indicate the complex understanding of mathematics that he is constructing for himself. When given the numbers 7, 5, 3, and 6 to add, Tyrone answered very quickly, "Twelve and nine is twenty-one." He had automatically broken the problem into two simpler addition problems, and then combined those answers to set up a new one.

"How did you know 12 plus 9 equals 21, Tyrone?" he was asked.

Interestingly, Tyrone's explanation does not even include the number 12. "Eleven plus nine is twenty because if you have a number [sic] like one and nine, you're going to have to get ten or one thousand or something like that. The number you get has to have a zero with it. So 11 plus 9 is 20. I took away that 1 to get the 11. I added it back and it was 21." Though roundabout, Tyrone's procedure and subsequent explanation indicate a finely tuned number sense and growing understanding of the properties of addition.

On a later occasion, Tyrone was given this story problem: "Juanita has 46 stickers in her sticker book. The book holds 75 stickers. How many more stickers can Juanita put in her book?" Without delay, he wrote the problem 75 – 46 vertically and then figured the correct answer, 29.

When asked how he got 29, Tyrone began a very complicated answer that appears indicative of his "number sense." (One actually must read his explanation several times to grasp what he is saying.) "Twenty plus forty-six is sixty-six," he began. "Then I added a 9 plus the 20 and it was 29. Because 6 is more than 5." He pointed to the 6 in 46 and continued, "If this was a 5, then I would have picked 30 because 10 plus 5 is 15, so 9 plus 6 is 15. I needed to get the 5 right there and then I needed to get the whole answer." As in many of his other solutions, Tyrone found a way to work with a multiple of ten. He knew that 20 added to 46 would get him as close to 75 as possible without going over. If the problem involved 45 instead of 46, he explained, he could have added 30 to make 75. Quickly and intuitively he had devised a process to help him arrive at a solution.

Tyrone likes to count by tens. In a free moment between assessment tasks, he was overheard mumbling while pointing to a number chart. Asked what he was saying, he explained, "Oh, I'm just counting by tens," and proceeded to count, "Three, thirteen, twenty-three, thirty-three. . . ." Sheer mathematical enjoyment seems to provide an intrinsic motivation to explore numbers and their relationships.

When asked to count out seventeen chips one day, Tyrone got as far as "One, two, three," and then stopped, smiled, and returned the chips to the pile. "I know a better way," he said. Moving the chips into five piles of three with two left over, he counted, "Three, six, nine, twelve, fifteen, sixteen, seventeen." His next task involved counting twenty-six chips. "Let's see how I can count. I'm going to count by fives." He arranged the chips in groups of five and counted them easily, "Five, ten, fifteen. . . ." After reaching twenty-six, he began to count the piles. "I was just wondering how many piles of five there are in twenty-five," he explained when he was done, then added, "There are five." As he so often does, Tyrone took this task not one, but several steps beyond what was called for. The reward for his ongoing investigation of number relationships is the continued discovery of more and more complex mathematics concepts.

With Tyrone, the enjoyment of mathematics is always evident, and there is little doubt that it is fundamental to his math development. Whether Tyrone's math appreciation and performance are the direct result of his school's mathematics program or the manifestation of an innate mathematical aptitude is unimportant. The fact is, his talent and unorthodox procedures were not squelched by rigid, rule-directed mathematics instruction. He continues to have the desire to explore mathematics and dig deeply into every experience.

What's more, his enjoyment seems infectious. At one point, a boy named Gerard joined Tyrone's class and the two became good friends. Neither Gerard's background nor his actions would have suggested he was a creative mathematical thinker. In fact, he appeared uninterested in school and unprepared to tackle mathematics problems that required higher-level thinking skills. But after several months in the class, Gerard showed indications of a growing mathematics awareness that went far beyond any initial impressions.

In one assessment, Gerard was given the numerals 1, 2, 3, and 4 on separate cards. He was then asked to arrange these cards to make two double-digit numbers that, when added together, would equal the largest possible sum. One natural tendency with this problem is to make the largest possible number first (43), and add it to the next largest number possible (21), making the problem 43 + 21. This is just what Gerard did. The teacher checked to make sure this was Gerard's final answer, gathered up the cards, and began to prepare the materials for the next problem.

"Wait a minute!" interrupted Gerard. He wanted the cards back. Quickly he set them up to read 41 + 32.

"What made you change your mind?" asked the teacher.

"Well, I kept thinking. Four tens plus three tens is more than four tens plus two tens," he said. "And I knew it didn't matter how the ones were." A few months earlier, no one saw or expected this kind of thinking from Gerard, but now Gerard was on the move with math.

Gerard's story underscores the value of giving children adequate time to reflect on their work, and opportunities to share with each other. Given a timed pencil-and-paper task that only focused on right and wrong answers, Gerard would have been marked wrong when he was actually quite capable of getting the right answer. Moreover, no one would have realized the sophisticated ideas that eventually led him to solve the problem correctly.

It's impossible to know how much Gerard was influenced by his friendship with Tyrone, but it is very probable that Tyrone is learning mathematics in a setting where he has the potential to powerfully influence others with his mathematical thinking and self-confidence. Undeniably, a mathematics program that encourages children to think creatively, to express that thinking, and to share cooperatively with their classmates provides avenues of positive influence among its students.

Unfortunately, Gerard did not stay long in Tyrone's classroom. His family moved on to another school district, and he moved on to another math program. It is impossible to know what Gerard's future holds, or what influence his brief stay in this school will have on his mathematics development. It's also hard to know how many other Gerards sit in classrooms that do not spark an interest in mathematics, or how many Tyrones go unnoticed in programs that don't encourage creative thinking or support children's personal construction of understanding.

The capacity for creative mathematical thinking resides in virtually all young children, but it needs to be released and nurtured. This takes motivation, patience, and a mathematics program that is focused on the kinds of content and teaching approaches promoted by the

NCTM standards. "I don't care who tells me that Tyrone's ability to do math isn't something that this program created, that it's something that was in him all along," said one educator working with Tyrone. "I say to them, great! I'm glad that we didn't destroy it in him." Isn't this what all children deserve?

10
●●●●●●●●●

SOME QUESTIONS ANSWERED

We've seen how a child-centered program can help a student like Tyrone, but what about students who do not share his mathematical enthusiasm and interest?

All students learn when they are given the opportunity to construct their own understanding. Students who traditionally test low, those whose home and school backgrounds are not conducive to academic achievement, often flourish in programs that follow the NCTM standards.

Eddie is a child whose academic performance is weak, his achievement low. His environment outside of school is not conducive to learning. Eddie tests poorly on questions that require rote memory. His problems are made even more difficult by the fact that he has not learned to read. In a recent one-on-one assessment, he appeared fatigued and complained that sirens had kept him awake the night before. Explaining a far-out answer he wrote on a pencil-and-paper problem, he said, "When I don't know something I just write down a number I haven't used in a long time." Without a doubt, Eddie is a student who would be headed for academic failure in a traditional system.

Fortunately for Eddie, his teacher encourages good thinking as much as right answers and has helped him develop a mathematical sense. His understanding is strengthened and reinforced through teaching strategies that incorporate manipulative materials and student discussions, but his vocabulary is still weak and he often needs direct, one-to-one discussions to aid his mathematics progress.

Early in his second-grade year, Eddie's teacher set up a unique geometry assessment, one designed to show analysis and reasoning skills rather than name recognition. In this activity, one pattern block was placed on the table and three others were tucked away in cloth bags. The children were asked to reach in the bags, feel each shape, and identify which shape matched the one on the table. Then they had to explain what attributes about the shapes led them to make their decision. This process encouraged the children to focus on the characteristics rather than the names of the shapes. Eddie did very well. He was able to use this tactile experience to identify the shapes and was guided in his discussion to explain his selection.

Had Eddie been asked simply to identify a rectangle or triangle, he may or may not have given the right answer. In either case, he probably would have been guessing. He does not have the requisite vocabulary. But given the opportunities to focus on the attributes that made up the shapes and the relationships among these characteristics, Eddie was successful. Because he was thinking about the characteristics that are used to classify shapes, he was able to explain why one shape matched the rectangle and was not a parallelogram, or a circle, or a square. This is mathematics, not just rote memorization of facts and names learned from a few pictures, so in some ways, Eddie is ahead of his contemporaries, who are merely attaching names to visual cues.

It's clear that using manipulative materials will help the child who has difficulty understanding math concepts, but it can be time-consuming to use these methods for the whole class. Doesn't the fact that the students can complete the problems with pencil and paper indicate mastery of the concept?

In today's busy classrooms, it's easy to see why teachers might worry about the extra time it takes to incorporate hands-on strategies in math programs above kindergarten. However, allowing children the opportunity to construct their understanding is never a waste of time. The underlying goal of any mathematics program in the primary grades should be to lay a strong foundation so that all students will be prepared to meet the demands of later mathematics instruction and be able to relate mathematical ideas to real-world events.

Children can often complete arithmetic problems using traditional algorithms, but does this achievement on a pencil-and-paper test truly indicate mastery of a concept? Not always. Jamal is a second grader who, in a pencil-and-paper assessment, correctly solved this double-digit addition problem with no regrouping:

$$\begin{array}{r} 72 \\ + 13 \\ \hline \end{array}$$

Later, he was given the same problem, but this time he was asked to demonstrate the solution with base-ten blocks. He *constructed* the numbers correctly, using longs for the tens and single units for the ones, and it looked like he fully understood the process. However, when he went to name the number for the answer, he counted each block as one, regardless of whether it was a long or single unit. This time, he reported the answer as 13. Jamal, as it turns out, did not fully understand place value in the operation. He was just adding the digits in their columns as though both columns were ones.

Jamal's incomplete understanding was masked by his pencil-and-paper work on a simple problem. He did not fully understand place value, so he could not model it with the base-ten blocks. He relied instead on rote memory of single-digit addition facts. However, math without meaning does not withstand the test of time. Jamal may be able to pass through the early grades, but unless he develops a more complete mathematical understanding, he will be lost when he encounters more complex mathematics.

Ms. McLeod, Jamal's teacher, discovered that many of the students in her class needed more opportunities to build place value understanding and so she decided to provide more experiences that would help move them forward with this important concept. She made manipulatives available but also made sure that the children recorded on paper what they had done with the manipulatives.

First, she had the children solve story problems that involved the kind of two-digit numbers that they needed to understand. She helped them record their work and had them talk about why it made sense to them. For example, she gave them this problem: Jenette had 56 stamps. Her grandmother gave her 17 more stamps. How many stamps did Jenette have then? Before reading the problem aloud, she gave them sets of unifix cubes, some of which had been made up into sticks of ten, to use if they wanted to. Some children used the unifix cubes to solve the problem, others worked on paper. Some counted by ones, but often got confused because 56 is such a large number to count. It was the children who used the prepared unifix cubes who solved the problem most easily.

When the students had completed the problem, Ms. McLeod called them together to share their results. There were several different answers, so she asked how they might check to see which was the real one; they couldn't all be right. Students shared strategies and decided on the correct answer. She then asked them to compare their strategies. How were they alike and different? Which seemed easier to do? Most children agreed that using the cubes that were made up into tens was easier than counting by ones. But Ms. McLeod did not stop there. She modeled for the children how to record with paper and pencil what they had done with the cubes. This activity helped the children build their understanding of place value and it started them on the road to developing efficient procedures for adding any two-digit numbers that made sense to them.

Ms. McLeod knew that a variety of experiences would be the best way to strengthen that place value concept, so the next day she had her students do a counting activity, where they took turns counting by five. They predicted what the final number counted would be, and they discussed why the numbers all ended in either 5 or 0. When this was finished, she asked them to count by five again, but this time they would start with the number 3, so that the count would go, 3, 8, 13, 18, 23, 28, 33. Again, they discussed the pattern, why the numbers all ended in 3 or 8, and what made it easy or hard to count that way. As time went by, Ms McLeod engaged the class in a variety of experiences that caused them to think about place value, skip counting, and grouping numbers in various ways—all aimed at helping the children make sense of multidigit numbers.

It is easy to assume student mastery when children perform well on pencil-and-paper tasks, but what about their ability to perform in real-world situations? Students need to see how the symbols on paper relate to real problems, real objects. They need multiple opportunities with problems and materials that help build mathematical understanding, and they need to record what they are doing with the materials so they can gradually develop the numeric skills that represent their work. Rather than being taught an algorithm that someone else says is the "right" way, students need to first construct their own procedures—procedures that have meaning to them and can be replicated and modified to meet the demands of more difficult mathematical tasks.

It's hard not to worry about children giving wrong answers and developing wrong procedures. Doesn't this reinforce misunderstandings?

Right answers are important and necessary in any mathematics program, therefore we *do* want to worry about children developing incorrect and inefficient procedures and giving wrong answers.

Failure to help students correct those procedures and answers could reinforce misunderstanding. In programs that value understanding as much as right answers, teachers reinforce whatever right thinking the child has exhibited and addresses wrong thinking.

It is important to remember that correct answers do not always represent right thinking, nor are they always the result of mathematical understanding. Conversely, incorrect answers do not necessarily indicate total lack of mastery, and must be handled in a manner that helps children build skills, understanding, and confidence. As many teachers have noted, it is easier to value right thinking than wrong answers. Asking children who give correct answers to explain their thinking enables teachers to identify those areas of a concept or procedure that a child understands and those that he does not. The teacher can then support what the child understands and help get the child back on track through careful questioning and well-planned activities.

It's important that teacher-generated questions lead to discussions rather than to single correct answers. Asking students to explain how they arrived at an answer often leads to self-correction, especially in situations where a single error has been made. Allowing more "wait time" often provides a student with an opportunity to explain his thinking clearly and to correct any faulty processes (as with Kevin in Chapter 7 and Gerard in Chapter 9). This process often results in a productive line of thinking that is more powerful than the one he initially used. Some students may need manipulatives to model their thinking, or they might need to start with a similar problem that involves easier numbers in order to focus on how they are solving the problem without worrying about numbers that are too challenging.

Children gain confidence when they are encouraged to prove their answer by explaining their thinking. No longer dependent on the teacher for verification, they grow to believe that they control the math, rather than that the math controls them. Consequently, the children begin to enjoy math more and will even strive toward a greater understanding of it.

This whole approach—just letting children use strategies such as manipulatives or drawings to invent their own ways to do math—sounds pretty unstructured. Where does the teaching come in?

The teacher's role in classrooms implementing the NCTM standards is vital to student development. Helping children control their own learning requires that teachers plan, structure, guide, and continually evaluate the mathematics program. While it's true that children must construct knowledge for themselves, it is the teacher who establishes what the goals for the mathematics program will be and how to help the student move toward these goals. He will map out the plans for the year, design appropriate units, develop meaningful situations for daily lessons, ask good questions, focus on student thinking, and use evidence of student thinking to plan the next lessons so that they will be as effective as possible, always keeping in mind the fact that children construct understanding rather than absorb it.

The teacher maintains control of how the mathematics in each day's activity is developed. He places children in meaningful situations that require problem-solving skills. These might include manipulative materials, class-developed projects, or real-world situations, but each will incorporate circumstances in which children confront a problem and develop their own solutions using their background knowledge.

Designing classroom situations is only the beginning of the teacher's role. He then must maximize an experience by developing its mathematics potential. Students need to make connections between their experiences and the math concepts. Student-student, teacher-student, and whole-group discussions help to bring out the mathematics. Teachers ask the questions that connect the experiences to math and forge a link between previously acquired math concepts and those currently being addressed. It is these connections that build the knowledge structure necessary for a strong mathematics foundation.

Using manipulative materials without making these connections is not an effective instructional strategy, for if the bridge between the manipulatives and math concepts is not built, students can wind up learning two procedures that they do not perceive to be related—the manipulatives provide one procedure, the symbols become the other. If, for example, a teacher has his students subtracting with base-ten blocks, but never connects the block subtraction with subtraction using numeric symbols, he has created a burden for the children rather than a support. The children have memorized one set of rules for using the blocks and another set for the using the symbols. Without guidance, they may never see the relationship.

The teacher's role in a standards-based classroom cannot be overstated. It involves observing student thinking and using it to carefully plan effective lessons that involve well-organized activities. While students are participating in their activities, the teacher is moving about the class asking questions and offering support. He ensures that class discussions establish strong links between experience and concept, and he makes sure all children are making these connections. There is evidence that children who invent their own ways of doing problems are mathematically stronger than those who don't. This probably applies whether or not the teacher eventually has the children learn the traditional algorithms. In one study, children who invented their own procedures understood place value better, were more flexible in transferring their ideas to new types of problems, and made fewer systematic errors than children who were taught traditional algorithms directly (Carpenter et al. 1997). "Systematic errors" are ones that relate to performing a rote procedure incorrectly, such as adding both the numerators and denominators when adding fractions. If we think about the kind of reasoning that children must use when inventing procedures of their own, these findings make a lot of sense, and they indicate strategies that are worth encouraging.

What are some hints for conducting productive class discussions?

It is not always easy to meet the needs of twenty-five students in a large-group discussion, and it is the skillful teacher indeed who is able to balance the needs of each student against those of an entire class. However, many teachers have discovered certain guidelines that can help facilitate productive group discussions.

First, it is important to establish the goal of group process. If the goal is only to hear correct answers, then the teacher need only call on the children raising their hands, listen to their answers, and move on to the next question. But in classrooms where the same students raise their hands all the time, the same students get called on all the time, and all the interaction between teacher and group is with those few students. The rest of the class remains passive and many students may not even participate mentally. Hearing no incorrect answers, it is easy for a teacher to interpret the class response as an indication that it is safe to move on to new content, when in fact, many children may still not understand the content just presented.

To help every child develop mathematical understanding and, at the same time, to improve social and language skills, many teachers

Some Effective Inquiries

Tell me what you were thinking.

How did you get your answer?

How can you decide if it is right?

Does it seem to make sense? Why or why not?

Try to write a problem that uses those numbers.

Try to act it out.

Use these (blocks) to model what you did.

How is the strategy with the blocks like the paper-and-pencil method?

Draw a picture of what happened and see if that helps.

How are these two strategies alike? How are they different?

Which way do you think will work best for you? Why?

Figure 10–1

may call initially on the quiet or reticent students. These children may need extra time and support to participate. They can be called on early in the discussion, before the obvious ideas have been given, and allowed ample time to reflect and respond. Using questions that have more than one right answer or that expect children to express their thinking encourages many children to "get in on the action" (see Figure 10–1).

When a student gives an answer, it is important to have him explain how he arrived at the answer. Correct answers might be the result of an intuitive flash or faulty reasoning. On the other hand, incorrect answers may represent only a minor error in an otherwise logical procedure. When children explain their thinking, teachers can uncover the logic behind the answer and students can clarify and confirm their own thinking.

Teachers often struggle with how to handle the student who gets stuck explaining an answer. Asking the child if she needs help, or even allowing her to call on a friend for assistance, sends the message that she is incapable of solving the problem herself. When the child feels that her teacher and classmates trust her to solve the problem and will allow her the time and support she needs, she is encouraged to try new ideas without fear of failure. Given time and confidence, she may develop a workable solution.

No matter how long the "wait time," however, some students simply will not be able to come up with an appropriate response. Perhaps they lack sufficient background knowledge or are confused by some element of the problem. Maybe they need the freedom to think longer than the group can afford during the discussion time. Chris Valentine confronted this situation when Danielle set out to explain her complicated grouping system, as described in Chapter 3. Realizing that Danielle needed more time, Chris moved on, returning to Danielle only when it appeared she was ready to continue. In situations in which it is less apparent that the student is ready or able to arrive at an answer or explain a solution, Chris returns to the student another day. She notes these incidents often indicate specific weaknesses that need to be addressed through further classroom activities.

Teachers who base their instruction on the NCTM standards believe that group discussions are essential to helping students clarify their thinking, establish mathematical procedures, and see math concepts from a variety of perspectives. All of these benefits work to strengthen concepts and skills. Group discussions provide closure for almost any kind of classroom experience and offer teachers valuable opportunities to assess the effectiveness of the lesson.

Doesn't taking the time to have one child explain her thinking rob the rest of the students of time they need?

Not really. Harold Cutler, who taught an intermediate elementary grade, presented a number of problems to his class. "I want you to pick two problems that you can do in your head," he told them. "Be prepared to share your method."

The first child who raised her hand explained, "I picked 35 minus 21. I thought 5 minus 1 is four and 3 minus 2 is 1, so the answer is 14."

"Okay," said Mr. Cutler, "did anyone else do it a different way?"

"I said 35 minus 20 is 15 and 21 is 1 more than 20, so the answer must be 14," offered a second student.

"Did anyone do it a different way?" the teacher continued.

"I thought 35 is 5 times 7 and 21 is 3 times 7. I subtracted the 3 from 5 and got 2, and 2 times 7 is 14," explained Brandy.

Although Brandy's unique approach involves mathematical procedures most elementary students would be unfamiliar with, it exemplifies the value of allowing the time for students to share their thinking. None of the other children, and few adults, would have thought of Brandy's unique method, but upon hearing her solution, some might think, "Maybe I can do that too."

Each individual approaches math problems in a slightly different way. Sharing these approaches not only concretizes procedures for the speaker, it also broadens the possibilities for those listening. Tyrone, the young mathematician in Chapter 9, has a keen mathematical awareness. His own conceptual understanding is deep rooted, but his approach is often unconventional. Although he is able to develop meaningful procedures for himself, he once told a teacher he likes to hear his classmates' explanations because he often hears things he would not have thought of.

Teachers must continually balance the time required for productive class discussion with the need to move the students on to the next unit of study. Group discussions also help students who have fallen behind for one reason or another to catch up and help children develop deeper understanding. Providing students sufficient time to develop this deeper understanding pays dividends as children move through the grades by decreasing the likelihood that they will need remedial work in later years.

What about the children who just are not "good" at math?

Schools, teachers, and parents need to foster the belief that *all* students can succeed at mathematics. Many people attribute the higher achievement of Japanese students to a greater natural mathematical ability. In reality, one factor in their mathematical achievement appears to be parental attitude. Japanese parents tend to feel that mathematics is a difficult subject, but with hard work any child can succeed. American parents, on the other hand, often feel that to succeed in mathematics, children need a natural ability or special talent (Stevenson, Lee, and Stigler 1986). Recent evidence also seems to indicate that Japanese teachers focused lessons on fewer problems solved in greater depth, followed by shared strategies and discussion. American teachers, on the other hand, tended to have their students solve many problems in superficial ways (Stigler and Hiebert 1999).

Allowing children the time and opportunity to construct their own mathematics understanding will help them develop a strong foundation. This, in turn, will help them as they progress through more complex mathematics courses in future grades, regardless of what the initial perception of their "ability" may be.

Children who feel they are not good in math often have not been provided with enough opportunities to experience success. They may not have been presented with situations in which they could connect their personal experiences to school mathematics. Virtually all schoolchildren functioning in our school systems have the ability to achieve mathematically in their own time and in their own way. It is the teacher's mission to help each child realize her math potential through successful completion of activities at her own level, free of stress and anxiety.

"Math anxiety" just seems a part of our culture. How can we keep it from affecting our students?

Many adults, including some teachers, feel anxious about mathematics. Teacher math anxiety, parental math anxiety, and student math anxiety are related; if teachers or parents feel anxious about math, they are probably going to communicate this to their students. Math anxiety probably originates from the kind of mathematics programs so many adults experienced as students themselves— programs that emphasized getting the right answer and teacher- or curriculum-prescribed rules. These rarely nurtured individual thinking and confidence.

Jannelle Riviera has taught in primary grades for seventeen years. She chose early childhood education, she admits, because of her anxieties about math and science. She was fairly sure she could handle the first-, second-, and even third-grade curricular content, but did not feel capable of teaching more difficult concepts. Once she began teaching, she restricted her mathematics program to "math time" and never veered from the prescribed path. Then her school joined a project that helped teachers implement an NCTM standards-based program. She knew it was time to rethink her attitudes toward mathematics. She was surprised by the results.

Rather than being the chore that she expected, Ms. Riviera has found that following the NCTM recommendations actually provides her relief from her long-standing anxiety; that is, when she gives her students the time and opportunity to construct their own mathematics knowledge, she feels less pressured to be the "expert." She now sees her responsibility as one of placing children in situations in which they can work individually or together to solve problems that will move them toward the intended math concepts.

"I don't have all the answers," she explains. "But I do need to provide a situation in which the children are going to be motivated to explore and discover." Sometimes it's difficult to accept that you don't

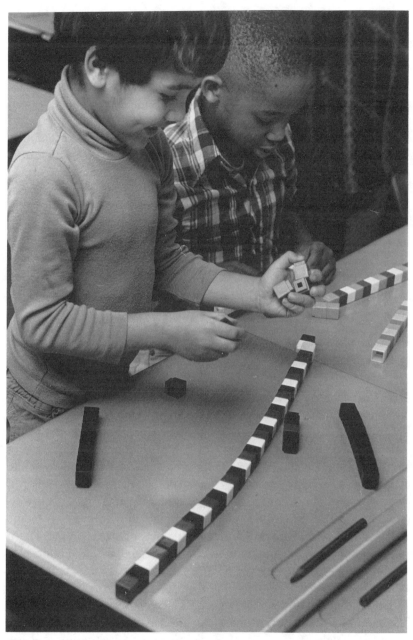

Allowing children the time and opportunity to construct their own mathematics understanding will help them develop a strong foundation.

THINKING LIKE MATHEMATICIANS

have to know it all, but the fact is, even when you do, you should restrain yourself from giving solutions so that students can discover these for themselves. One mathematics educator has suggested, "Never say anything a kid can say" (Reinhart 2000).

It is always easier to feel that you know all of the answers to every possible question the students could ask. Sometimes teachers even try to organize the lesson so that the questions that the children are likely to ask will not stray beyond their own levels of understanding. This can instill false confidence, allowing teachers to believe that they can always successfully guide students to desired learning outcomes. Even if this were the case, this practice is not in the best interest of student learning. Teachers should encourage children to ask any questions about the mathematics. When questions arise that the teacher cannot answer, she can freely admit it and say something like "Let's see if we can work together to find that answer," "Maybe there's another teacher who can help," or "Maybe we can locate a solution in a book." These responses let the students know that everyone continues to learn; no one knows all of the answers. Teachers can learn much about mathematics, as well as about their students, by listening to what those students are thinking as they solve problems.

How can I help students solve story problems?

For years children were taught to look for "clues" or "key words" in story problems. These were words that told them whether they needed to add, subtract, multiply, or divide. And in the neat world of textbook math, problems were always written to follow these specific rules. The objective was a "right answer," not an understanding of the problem. However, real-life problems do not work this way. Students need to develop the means to understand both the problems and the math within the problems to find appropriate solutions. There simply is no magic formula for solving problems; asking children to rely on universal rules discourages them from thinking for themselves about mathematics problems.

One classroom displayed a wall chart labeled "Clue Words for Story Problems." Listed on the chart were a series of "clues" and their meanings, including "*all together* means . . . *add*." Although that frequently is the case, the real world does not usually come equipped with clue words. What happens when a child who relies on this chart encounters a problem like the following: Terry collects trading cards.

For her birthday, Daniel gave her twelve cards. Now she has forty-five all together. How many cards did Terry have before her birthday? Telling students to look for clue words is essentially telling them not to think. That is certainly not an appropriate goal for school mathematics programs.

The best mathematicians use a variety of techniques to help them understand and solve problems. Children, too, need to develop a repertoire of strategies and techniques that will work for them. Teachers can use ideas similar to those presented in the reading curriculum when promoting critical-thinking skills in their students.

In reading instruction, children are often taught dramatization, visualization, and prediction strategies to assist their comprehension. Whether the goal is reading comprehension or mathematical problem solving, dramatization helps children understand the characters and events in that story. Consequently, the story takes on more meaning for the reader. Similarly, manipulating concrete materials that represent story components allows children to model situations and better understand problems. Visualization techniques also help concretize story ideas. Students can organize their thoughts graphically by making a web, matrix, drawing, or time line. Prediction helps develop a context for reading and similarly, in math, the use of prediction (sometimes in the form of estimation) provides a basis for finding logical solutions or judging a solution's reasonableness once it is found.

Sometimes the best problem solvers are those who take full ownership of a story problem. Teachers can make stories meaningful for children by incorporating events and ideas that students can value and identify with. In turn, these problems become inherently interesting and encourage students to seek solutions. Having students write problems for each other can increase the level of ownership as well as interest.

Enrico, a second grader, was completely distracted as he waited to begin an oral math assessment at school. He spent his time alternately sliding under his chair and climbing on top of his desk. He gave every indication that he was not listening.

"Tiffany has three snakes . . ." began the teacher.

"Snakes!" interrupted Enrico. "SNAKES!" He was delighted to hear a question about his favorite creatures and discover that his classmate Tiffany had a collection of them.

His teacher continued, "Malcolm has some snakes too."

"Malcolm! MALCOLM!" Enrico interrupted again. "He's my best friend."

Enrico's body language seemed to suggest that he was not paying attention to the task at hand. In a more traditional setting, his teacher might have been tempted to reprimand him for being so disruptive. But this teacher realized that Enrico's energy could be focused when learning situations are meaningful.

Enrico is a child who really brings life to math stories. This problem became real to him because he could associate with his friends Tiffany and Malcolm and value their collection of snakes. Enrico went on to solve the problem and was ready for another.

Some children actually alter stories to create personal meaning. Nikki, a kindergartner, was asked, "If you have twelve cupcakes and want to share them with two friends, how many cupcakes will each child have?" Before she answered, she was asked to restate the question. "Well," Nikki began, "I have twelve cupcakes and I want to have a party. I ask Jessie and Amanda to come to my party . . ." She reconstructed the story to suit her own needs and then solved it. Many children have difficulty with this type of problem because they can't decide whether they should be counted in the group sharing the cupcakes. Rethinking the problem as a personal experience is one way to avoid this error.

Nikki is used to personalizing story problems. Her teacher encourages students to create meaning from the story problems in their textbooks. In pairs, students read different story problems and decide how they can communicate their problem to the rest of the class. They might retell it in their own words, dramatize it, or model it with concrete objects. Then they describe how they would determine the solution.

Children come to school already able to solve problems. The teacher's task, then, is to help them retain that ability and extend it to new types of problems. When children can identify with the characters and content of the story, they better understand the problem and are likely to be more efficient problem solvers. The more often story problems are used as the basis for mathematics lessons, the better children become at solving them. When teachers see children are struggling with a problem, they might decide to revise the problem, using smaller numbers so that it is easier to solve, and return to the original problem once the students understand the problem-solving process. Children also benefit when given a choice of several different types of problems in a variety of contexts. Not only does this allow them to start with problems they feel comfortable with, it also provides opportunities for them to listen to and learn from the strategies that others used on the problems that they decided not to solve. Drawing, using graphic organizers, and acting out the story are also powerful tools for children to use when deciding how to solve a problem.

Isn't it better to have children grouped by ability?

Often, teachers do not have any control over the students assigned to their particular class. Some schools evenly distribute students across classrooms; others assign teachers more homogenous groupings. Whatever the case, there is usually a range of ability and achievement within a class, and with it comes the opportunity to incorporate both homogenous and heterogeneous in-class groupings. Fluidity of grouping allows teachers to change group assignments weekly, by subject, or with each activity.

There is no clear evidence that ability grouping improves learning, even for highly able students. In fact, there is evidence that ability grouping can have a negative effect on average- and low-achieving students. There may be indications that the very highly gifted benefit from ability grouping, but even these results are mixed. Evidence of long-term differences seems especially difficult to find (Secada 1992, 650–2). Conversely, whether due to ability or lack of motivation, lower-achieving students tend to have more discipline problems. Assigning them all into one group concentrates disruptions and virtually ensures that these students will lose even more ground. There may be no one in the group to demonstrate appropriate ways of expressing creative thinking or model acceptable classroom behavior.

Achievement levels in the early grades do not always reflect the ability to learn, but rather, indicate enriched early childhood experiences or differing levels and rates of maturity. Heterogeneous grouping in the primary grades helps to keep opportunities of advancement equitable while children mature and builds a common history of experience. See Figures 10–2, 10–3, 10–4, 10–5, and 10–6 on the following pages.

Despite fears to the contrary, heterogeneous grouping rarely holds back the more able students. In fact, moving very bright children ahead through the curriculum until they reach the point at which they get frustrated serves no purpose, especially in elementary grades. When children are rushed quickly into the abstract, they often encounter a narrow channel of instruction. At some point in the future, they will need to look at ideas from a variety of perspectives, and if

Figure 10–2 *Assignments that allow children to make choices and seek their own level of comfort are particularly useful in heterogeneous groups. Here, second-grade students were provided with a set of items they could "purchase" at the prices indicated, and then asked to write story problems. Each child completed the assignment at his or her own level of understanding.*

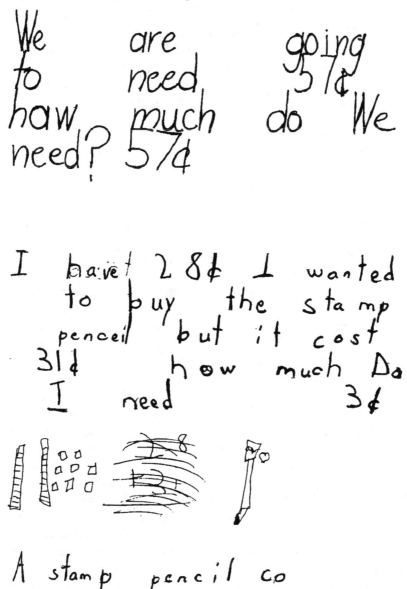

We are going to need 57¢
how much do We
need? 57¢

I have 28¢ I wanted
to buy the stamp
pencel but it cost
31¢ how much Do
I need 3¢

A stamp pencil co

Figure 10–3

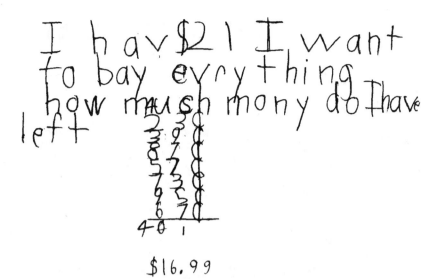

I hav $2 I I want to bay eyrything how mush mony do I have left

$16.99

Figure 10–4

I had 98¢ I 2 bunney

I had 98¢ I bot bins bunney it costs 82¢ I have I got 16¢ back

Figure 10–5

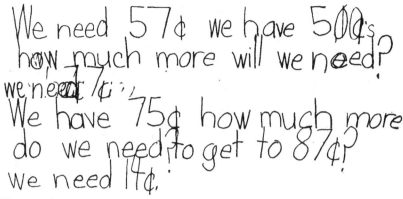

We need 57¢ we have 50¢'s how much more will we need?
we need 7¢.
We have 75¢ how much more do we need to get to 87¢?
We need 14¢.

Figure 10–6

they haven't had the opportunity to do that in elementary school, they could face serious trouble when required to do it in later years.

In groups where children work together cooperatively, students learn from each other. Heterogeneous groups offer a real mix of ideas, strengths, talents, and learning and reporting styles. Few children are unable to contribute something to the group process in a cooperative learning situation. For example, those who are slower at reading and writing are often very verbal. Children who intuitively reach solutions can learn from those who develop procedures step by step.

Tyrone, the highly able math student so often discussed in this text, is a product of frequent heterogeneous group experiences. His role in any mixed group would undoubtedly benefit the other children. He is able to articulate math processes, explaining and justifying each step along the way. But the benefits of mixed-ability grouping are hardly one-sided. Rather then holding him back, Tyrone's group experiences enrich him. He enjoys listening to other children explain how they did things in ways that he would have never thought of. Even though Tyrone is very able, there are always ways to approach a problem that he hasn't yet considered. Seeing those other ways and relating them to his own is beneficial and enriching to Tyrone.

Sometimes, it is useful to group students together who have gained common skills and understandings. For example, initial work in a unit on fractions may show that some students understand skills and concepts that other children have not yet achieved at the second-grade level. These students may be grouped together and assigned problems that challenge them while most groups in the class are working on beginning skills and concepts. Differentiating for levels of maturity or experience, moving some children ahead while others remain on a selected topic, can benefit all students. However, it is important to keep these groups flexible. Children sometimes experience rapid changes in the early grades, both in physical and mental maturity.

Some educators believe that with carefully crafted instructional planning, problems inherent in heterogeneous groupings can be minimized or avoided. For example, the teacher can assign a variety of tasks that require different levels of skill and/or concept development. The teacher can encourage the group to let each child work on a manageable portion of the overall task and have the total group share responsibility for the completed *set* of tasks.

Here is a summary of some ideas for making heterogeneous classes work well:

- Don't predetermine groups; regularly revise student groupings to reflect the current needs, strengths, and emerging abilities.
- Introduce new content to all students. To the extent possible, base the new ideas on background knowledge that the whole class is likely to have, so that all can have initial success.
- Allow students who understand to assist their peers. Research indicates that when children help others learn, they reinforce their own conceptual understanding. Often, explaining a process to another child helps them identify and correct their own misunderstandings.
- Call on *all* students, not just those who always raise their hands.
- Ask questions that cause children to share their thinking, not just an answer.
- Adjust the number size in the problems up or down to meet students where they are, while keeping the type of problem the same.
- Challenge students with two-step story problems when appropriate. A problem that requires the student to do addition first, then to subtract, is more difficult than one that requires only one operation.
- Change the level of difficulty of problems. ("Jan had 7 and Alice gave her 3 more; how many does she have now?" is easier than "Jan had 7 and Alice gave her some more; now she has 10. How many did Alice give her?")
- Offer problems or activities at varying levels of difficulty and allow children to choose those that they want to do, always encouraging choices that challenge.
- Use story problems reflecting the background knowledge of the students.
- Encourage invention of procedures.
- Have children create problems to share with their classmates.

What about homework?

Homework can play an important role in the math program. When approached constructively, it helps students to think about mathematics outside of the classroom and gets parents involved in their children's education.

Often the biggest problem with homework arises from parents who expect to see their children bring home the same kind of math homework they did when they were in school. However, drill-and-practice worksheets or textbook assignments rarely contribute to mathematics awareness outside of school. Some homework will be for practice, but it is the student who needs the practice, not the parent, and even practice should be accompanied by explanations of "why" and "what."

Parents need to know what the mathematics program is about so that they will understand the types of homework assigned. Early in the school year, teachers can explain in a letter to parents what they should expect their children to be doing for homework, and why the teacher believes in these assignments. This is also a good opportunity to let parents know how they can help their children progress mathematically, what types of home experiences to offer, and what types of questions to ask their children.

Many schools conduct "family math programs" at times that parents, siblings, and caregivers can attend. These activities serve several purposes. They convey the message that mathematics is important, and they provide teachers and administrators an opportunity to explain the new views in math education and why school and home assignments may not look like those the parents have experienced. They also offer a format that allows teachers to model for parents various ways to interact with children when they do math homework.

Computational homework, done within the context of a meaningful activity, might involve other curricular areas or reinforce content being covered in school. Students might write a story that incorporates math concepts. They might count or measure the doors in their home or graph the number of rooms. They could even take a math game home from school and teach it to the family, or they could develop a game at home to bring to school. Parents and students can work as partners in activities and then discuss and record together what they have done. Teachers must help parents understand that the most beneficial approach they can take is to encourage the child to tell what he did in school and explain what he learned from it. Parents can have the child teach them the procedure he invented and explain why it works, or talk about the geometric shapes the class is working with.

Teachers should work with the caregivers of students who lag behind their classmates, suggesting ways that they can engage their children in activities that call for mathematical thinking. For example, cooking and meal preparation provide natural opportunities to discuss and use mathematics around the home. Baking requires counting, careful measurement, use of fractions, and a sense of time. Less structured activities occur every day: one-to-one correspondence involved in setting the table, dividing a plate of cookies into equal shares, or slicing a piece of toast into four equal parts and discussing the fraction of the original slice of bread that each part represents. Adults with access to computers can find more suggestions on the NCTM-developed website, www.figurethis.org.

What about using calculators and computers in the classroom?
Calculators and computers are part of the real world and are here to stay. These take away the drudgery of mathematics, improve efficiency, and increase accuracy of computation. This does not mean that students should not develop paper-and-pencil computational skills. Such skills are an important part of daily life. It does mean that there are times when any person would reach for the calculator because the problem is more complex than is reasonable to do with paper and pencil. Children should be able to use calculators in those same situations and, perhaps more important, should begin to make decisions as to when a situation is the type that is appropriate for calculator use.

Many times children are handed pages of drill-and-practice problems to compute. The students complete them, check them, and correct them, only to be handed more of the same, even when they have done the initial work correctly. "Why should we spend thousands of dollars to teach children to do poorly what a five-dollar machine can do well?" asked Judah Schwartz in a presentation at an NCTM conference in 1989.

The technology principle of the 2000 *Principles and Standards* states: "Technology is essential in teaching and learning mathematics; it influences the mathematics that is taught and enhances students' learning" (24). The value of technology in the primary-grade classroom is frequently overlooked and too often relegated to filling a gap in unstructured "free time" activity. It can, however, play an integral role in the mathematics curriculum.

Calculators are instructional tools as well as devices to improve computational efficiency. Students can use calculators to investigate number patterns and the effect of computational algorithms. Such investigations would often be impossible without the calculator. Used this way, calculators provide a dimension to the instructional program that could not be achieved with pencil and paper alone. Place value activities that use the calculator cause children to focus on the value of each digit in a number, rather than just the location of the digit. If a student wants to put a 6 in the hundreds place on paper, he need only know the location of that place. If the same task is performed on a calculator, then the student must enter the number 600 to get that 6 into the hundreds place— he must show the value, not just know the location.

One interesting second- through fifth-grade activity is to have the children work in groups with a calculator that they pretend has one or more broken keys. The broken keys can be an operation key, such as x, or any number key. The students are then challenged to solve a problem that would normally use that key or keys. They have to figure out how to work their way around the "broken" key and then record the steps that they used. This interesting activity provides a different kind of problem-solving experience that can require the students to think carefully about the meaning of the operations and how different numbers relate to one another.

Teachers can use computers with a whole class or for independent student work. One of the difficulties in using computers is the time required for the teacher to review and determine appropriate uses for the software; but by working together and sharing ideas and experiences, teachers can share information within and between schools about software, so that the time required of any individual teacher is minimized.

The NCTM standards emphasize the importance of reasoning. The abilities to do mental mathematics and estimation in flexible ways are very important skills when using technology, especially calculators and certain types of computer programs. Students should always be expected to decide if their answers are reasonable, whether those answers come from a calculator, a computer, or a paper-and-pencil procedure.

Students need to see classroom technology as a tool that helps them understand math better and extend their problem-solving capabilities, rather than as devices that excuse them from doing math. The potential exists for children to think that they should automatically use the computer or calculator whenever they are allowed, but they should learn that it is sometimes more efficient to use other methods such as mental math or pencil and paper—or perhaps estimation when they don't need an exact answer. Students should be asked to explain how and why they used a calculator, and then justify that decision, just as they would explain and justify any problem-solving technique.

In a nutshell, what are some of the most important things I can do to implement the standards of NCTM in my classroom?

1. Develop the mathematics through meaningful situations and problems that children can solve using their background experience, perhaps using manipulative materials or other means to model the story and its solution.

2. Encourage children to invent their own ways to solve problems and use these to move the children to more efficient procedures with understanding, perhaps including a traditional procedure if that is desired. Whether using an invented procedure or a traditional one, children should have computational procedures that lead to correct answers, that generalize to other problems of the same type, and that are eventually efficient. They should achieve this in ways that make sense to them and that allow them to "think like mathematicians."

3. Give children ample time to construct their understanding, reflect on their activities, and exchange ideas with peers and interested adults. Build new understanding on this constructed understanding.

4. Expect children to explain their thinking orally or in writing. Continually build good questioning strategies to bring out thinking. Listen to children's explanations and observe their work. Use the results of listening and observing to adjust future instruction so that students move forward smoothly in their understanding of mathematics.

How can I get a copy of the *Principles and Standards for School Mathematics?*
Write or call:

National Council of Teachers of Mathematics
1906 Association Drive
Reston, VA 22091-1953
Information: (703) 620-9840
Orders: (800) 235-7566
www.nctm.org

Works Cited

Ball, Deborah L. 1993. "Halves, Pieces, and Twoths: Constructing and Using Representational Contexts in Teaching Fractions." In *Rational Numbers: An Integration of Research,* edited by T. P. Carpenter, E. Fennema, and T. A. Romberg (157–96). Hillsdale, NJ: Lawrence Erlbaum Associates.

Carpenter, Thomas P., Megan Franke, Judith Jacobs, Elizabeth Fennema, and Susan Empson. 1997. "A Longitudinal Study of Invention and Understanding in Children's Multidigit Addition and Subtraction." *Journal for Research in Mathematics Education* 29 (1): 3–20. Reston, VA: National Council of Teachers of Mathematics.

Carpenter, T. P., and J. M. Moser. 1983. "The Acquisition of Addition and Subtraction Concepts." In *Acquisition of Mathematical Concepts and Processes,* edited by R. A. Lesh and M. Landau (7–44). Orlando, FL: Academic Press.

Clements, Douglas H., and Julie Sarama. 2000. "Predicting Pattern Blocks on and off the Computer." *Teaching Children Mathematics* March: 458–62. Reston, VA: National Council of Teachers of Mathematics.

Countryman, Joan. 1992. *Writing to Learn Mathematics: Strategies That Work*. Portsmouth, NH: Heinemann.

Empson, Susan B. 1995. "Using Sharing Situations to Help Children Learn Fractions." *Teaching Children Mathematics* October: 110–4. Reston, VA: National Council of Teachers of Mathematics.

Falkner, Karen P., Linda Levi, and Thomas P. Carpenter. 1999. "Children's Understanding of Equality: A Foundation for Algebra." *Teaching Children Mathematics* 6 (4): 232–7. Reston, VA: National Council of Teachers of Mathematics.

Fuson, Karen C. 1986. "Teaching Children to Subtract by Counting Up." *Journal for Research in Mathematics Education* 17 (3): 172–89. Reston, VA: National Council of Teachers of Mathematics.

Greeno, J. 1991. "Number Sense as Situated Knowing in a Conceptual Domain." *Journal for Research in Mathematics Education* 22 (3): 170–218. Reston, VA: National Council of Teachers of Mathematics.

Irons, Calvin, and Paul Trafton. 1992. *Moving into Math*. Grade 1. San Francisco: MIMOSA.

Kenney, Patricia A., and Edward A. Silver. 1997. *Results from the Sixth Mathematics Assessment of the National Assessment of Educational Progress.* Reston, VA: National Council of Teachers of Mathematics.

Mullis, Ina V. S., Michael O. Martin, Albert E. Beaton, Eugenio J. Gonzales, Dana L. Kelly, and Teresa A. Smith. 1997. *Mathematics Achievement in the Primary School Years: IEA's Third International Mathematics and Science Study (TIMSS)*. Chestnut Hill, MA: Boston College, TIMSS International Study Center.

National Commission on Excellence in Education. 1983. *A Nation at Risk: The Imperative for Educational Reform*. Washington, D.C.: U.S. Government Printing Office.

National Council of Teachers of Mathematics. 1989. *Curriculum and Evaluation Standards for School Mathematics*. Reston, VA: National Council of Teachers of Mathematics.

National Council of Teachers of Mathematics. 1990. *Professional Standards for Teaching Mathematics*. Reston, VA: National Council of Teachers of Mathematics.

National Council of Teachers of Mathematics. 1995. *Assessment Standards for School Mathematics.* Reston, VA: National Council of Teachers of Mathematics.

National Council of Teachers of Mathematics. 2000. *Principles and Standards for School Mathematics*. Reston, VA: National Council of Teachers of Mathematics.

National Science Board Commission on Precollege Education in Mathematics, Science, and Technology. 1983. *Educating Americans for the Twenty-First Century: A Plan for Action for Improving the Mathematics, Science, and Technology Education for All American Elementary and Secondary Students So That Their Achievement Is the Best in the World by 1995*. Washington, D.C.: National Science Foundation.

Reinhart, Steven. 2000. "Never Say Anything a Kid Can Say." *Mathematics Teaching in the Middle School* April: 478–83. Reston, VA: National Council of Teachers of Mathematics.

Schmidt, William H., C. McKnight, and S. Raizen. 1997. *A Splintered Vision: An Investigation of U.S. Science and Mathematics Education.* U.S. National Center for the Third International Mathematics and Science Study. Boston: Kluwer Academic Publishers.

Secada, W. G. 1992. "Race, Ethnicity, Social Class, Language, and Achievement in Mathematics." In *Handbook of Research on Mathematics Teaching and Learning*, edited by D. A. Grouws. New York: Macmillan.

Stevenson, H. W., S. Y. Lee, and J. Stigler. 1986. "Mathematics Achievement of Chinese, Japanese, and American Children." *Science* 231: 693–99.

Stigler, James W., and James Hiebert. 1999. *The Teaching Gap: Best Ideas from the World's Teachers for Improving Education in the Classroom.* New York: Free Press.

Thornton, C. A., and P. J. Smith. 1988. "Action Research: Strategies for Learning Subtraction Facts." *Arithmetic Teacher* 35 (8): 8–12.

Whitin, David J., Heidi Mills, and Timothy O'Keefe. 1990. *Living and Learning Mathematics: Stories and Strategies for Supporting Mathematical Literacy.* Portsmouth, N.H.: Heinemann.